WHY POLITICAL DEMOCRACY MUST GO

The Origins of Socialism in the United States

John Reed

WHY POLITICAL
DEMOCRACY
MUST GO

The Origins of Socialism
in the United States

Edited, with and Introduction by A.K. Brackob

GAUDIUM

Gaudium Publishing

Las Vegas ◊ Chicago ◊ Palm Beach

Published in the United States of America by
Histria Books
7181 N. Hualapai Way, Ste. 130-86
Las Vegas, NV 89166 USA
HistriaBooks.com

Gaudium Publishing is an imprint of Histria Books. Titles published under the imprints of Histria Books are distributed worldwide.

Library of Congress Control Number: 2021931625

ISBN 978-1-59211-099-5 (hardcover)
ISBN 978-1-59211-150-3 (softbound)
ISBN 978-1-59211-163-3 (eBook)

Table of Contents

Dedicated to
the American Worker

Introduction

Why Political Democracy Must Go is a collection of articles
on the American political system, originally published in an
eight-installment series in a short-lived weekly newspaper
called *The New York Communist* during May and June of
1919, in which John Reed traces the origins of Socialism in
the United States. Following his return from Russia, where
he gathered material for his well-known account of the
Russian Revolution, *Ten Days That Shook the World*, John
Reed became increasingly active in the Socialist movement
in the United States. Among other things, Reed served as
editor of *The New York Communist*, the voice of the left-wing
section of the Socialist Party of America in the New York
area.

John Silas Reed was an unlikely candidate to become a
radical leader, but the Harvard-educated journalist emerged
as one of the leading revolutionaries of his day. Born into an
upper-middle-class family in Portland, Oregon, on October
20, 1887, Jack Reed attended private schools in New Jersey
before entering Harvard University in 1906. At Harvard,
Reed met Professor Charles Copeland, who became his close

friend. He would later write that Cope, as he called him, "stimulated me to find color and strength and beauty in books and in the world and to express it."[1]

Reed's radicalism developed after he graduated from Harvard and became a journalist in New York. There he became the companion of the wealthy socialite Mabel Dodge who introduced him to one of the leaders of the I.W.W. (Industrial Workers of the World), William D. Haywood. As a result of this meeting, Reed covered the famous silk worker's strike in Patterson, New Jersey, where he was arrested for siding with striking workers. A year later, in November 1913, he was sent to cover the revolution in Mexico for *Metropolitan Magazine*. His reports from Mexico, where he accompanied the rebel army of Pancho Villa, won him praise in America, placing him among the leading journalists of his generation. As Bertram Wolfe noted: "His reports overflow with life and movement: simple, savage men, capricious cruelty, warm comradeship, splashes of color, bits of song, fragments of social and political dreams, personal peril, gay humor, reckless daring."[2] Reed's innate talent for description made his readers feel they were witnessing the events he recounted. His articles, published

---

[1]quoted in Bertram D. Wolfe, *Strange Communists I Have Known* (New York, 1967), p. 15.

[2]Wolfe, *Strange Communists*, p. 24.

in a volume later that same year under the title, *Insurgent Mexico*, cemented his reputation as a war correspondent.

While his romanticism, daring, and talent as a writer won him accolades, his experiences with the peasant armies of Pancho Villa further strengthened his growing socialist convictions. It must be remembered that for intellectuals of this generation, who had not yet experienced the atrocities that would be committed in its name, the ideals of Socialism held a romantic attraction, much the same way they do today for many who no longer have a historical sense of the tragedy of collectivism. In a world filled with poverty and injustice and overcome with a sense of stagnation, the dream of a socialist society attracted many followers — among them the American journalist John Reed. In many ways, he is a representative figure of his generation — a generation searching for its identity, famously referred to by Ernest Hemingway, quoting Gertrude Stein, as the "lost generation." His former classmate at Harvard, Walter Lippman, described him best when he wrote in *The New Republic* in 1914: "He is many men at once, and those who have tried to bank on some phase of him, to regard him as a writer, a correspondent, a poet, a revolutionist, or a lover, lose him. There is no line between the play of his fancy and his responsibility to fact; he is for the time the person he imagines himself to be."

Reed's opposition to World War I — which he saw as a struggle between capitalist interests — did not prevent him from traveling to Europe to cover the war on the Eastern front for *Metropolitan Magazine*. A romantic at heart, Reed yearned for adventure, and the war, he thought, would open up worlds of opportunities for him, just as it had in Mexico. Reed's travels in Eastern Europe formed the basis for his volume *The War in Eastern Europe*, published by Charles Scribner's Sons in New York in 1916. The book contained a series of drawings by Boardman Robinson, who accompanied Reed on his journey, meant to evoke the atmosphere the two Americans encountered in each of the countries described in the book. Still, he failed to recapture the romanticism he had experienced in Mexico amidst the staleness of trench warfare in Europe. As Bertram Wolfe pointed out, "His tour of duty as a European war correspondent was a disappointment to editors, friends, and to Jack himself."[3]

After returning to the United States, and dissatisfied with his travels in Eastern Europe, Reed again set out for Europe in August of 1917, this time inspired by the revolutionary changes taking place in Russia. It was here that he, together with his wife, Louise Bryant, bore witness to the Bolshevik revolution, which he believed would give birth to the socialist utopia he envisioned. Reed was not merely an observer of the historic events in Russia but also a participant in them. He whole-heartedly supported the

---

[3]Wolfe, *Strange Communists*, p. 25.

Bolshevik cause, working in the Bureau of International Revolutionary Propaganda for a time after the establishment of the Soviet regime. Before his return home, Leon Trotsky appointed him as the first Russian consul to the United States, but the designation was subsequently withdrawn due to fierce opposition from the American Embassy, as well as political infighting.

Reed returned to the United States in April of 1918 to face trial for sedition, along with Max Eastman and other former colleagues from *The Masses*. American customs officials initially confiscated the materials he brought back with him from Russia, but Reed eventually recovered them and proceeded to write his most famous book, *Ten Days that Shook the World*. It is this eyewitness account of the events that rocked Russia, which the British scholar Eric Homberger called, "perhaps the most remarkable account of a revolution ever to have been written by an eyewitness,"[4] that is John Reed's lasting claim to fame. It has been translated into numerous languages. The book's partisan nature is clear; Reed never attempts to hide his sympathy for the Bolshevik cause. Despite this, he manages to evoke the historic events in Russia during the fall of 1917 in such a way so as to transcend his own sense of partisanship and bring to life those heady times for generations of readers. Jack Reed fully utilizes the remarkable talent he had

---

[4]see Eric Homberger, "Messenger for Revolution," in *The Times Higher Education Supplement*, 17 March 1989, p.13.

demonstrated in his reports from Mexico in his account of the Bolshevik revolution. The book won praise from Lenin, and the Soviet leader even wrote a short preface to it.

Inspired by what he had experienced in Russia, Reed began to take a more active role in American politics, initially joining the Socialist Party of America. His close friend Max Eastman wrote: "He came home and not only defended the Bolsheviks in articles and speeches all over the country as others did — though few enough — but he laid aside all other hopes and rolled up his sleeves and went to work organizing an American Communist party dedicated to the overthrow of the American government and the capitalist system, and the institution of a soviet republic on these shores."[5] As with other socialist movements in the world in the wake of the Bolshevik revolution, the American left began to split into factions once the war had ended. It was during this time that Reed published his series *Why Political Democracy Must Go* in the *New York Communist*. In the summer of 1919, Reed was among those who broke away from the Socialist Party and founded the Communist Labor Party of America. At the same time, another socialist faction formed a rival Communist Party. As each side in this struggle between communist factions sought to gain legitimacy by obtaining recognition from the Comintern, John Reed was sent as the delegate of the Communist Labor

---

[5]Max Eastman, *Heroes I Have Known: Twelve Who Lived Great Lives* (New York: Simon & Schuster, 1942), p. 207.

Party to obtain recognition for the party in Moscow. He would never again set foot in the United States.

Failing to obtain recognition for his party from the Comintern, which ordered the two rival American communist factions to unite, Reed attempted to return home in the spring of 1920 amidst the civil war that raged in Russia at the time. He was arrested and imprisoned in Finland. Lenin and the Soviets intervened and secured his release, and he returned to Russia in June of 1920. Having temporarily abandoned plans to return to the United States, Reed worked in the Comintern, being selected as a member of the executive committee sent to the Congress of Peoples of the East in Baku. During this trip, he contracted typhus. When he returned to Moscow in September, he found that his wife, Louise Bryant, herself a remarkable journalist, had made the hazardous journey to Russia to join him. Their reunion was short-lived; Reed soon fell ill and died in October 1920. He was buried in the Kremlin wall, one of only three Americans to have been so honored by the Soviet regime.

Near the end of his life, as he saw the revolution begin to devour its own and stifle dissent, John Reed's enthusiasm for Bolshevism waned. He was a man of firm principle. As he watched the new Soviet leaders ever increasing abuses of power and their stifling of any dissent in the name of the revolution, his intellect rebelled. Max Eastman summed it up best when he wrote: "He wanted to live the life of this era *with* the arising classes and peoples of the earth in honest comradeship. He did not want to sit aloft in a new priesthood, a new cult of intellectual complaisance, knowing what is good for the masses, because Marx had explained it to him, and he had been superior enough to understand Marx, and was therefore justified in hoodwinking and cheating the masses, and arousing them any way he could to action called for by an esoteric conception of history."[6]

His frequent clashes with Zinoviev in the Comintern drained the Harvard educated intellectual. Reed was a romantic revolutionary by nature. As the Russian revolution morphed into a highly bureaucratic and oppressive regime that strived to snuff out the last vestiges of revolutionary fervor, he began to feel alienated by it. The English sculptress Claire Sheridan, who met him in Moscow shortly before he fell ill, wrote in her diary how out of place Reed seemed to her, "I understand the Russian spirit, but what strange force impels an apparently normal young man from the United States?"[7] Perhaps Bertram Wolfe answered that query and summed it up best went he wrote: "John Reed's spirit evades official control and goes its own characteristic way. It lives on in the record of his rebellious, adventurous,

[6]Eastman, *Heroes I Have Known: Twelve Who Lived Great Lives*, p. 233.

[7]Homberger, "Messenger for Revolution," p. 13.

generously romantic, perpetually immature, brave poet's life."[8]

***

Why Political Democracy Must Go is divided into eight parts. Part one is a brief introduction in which Reed simply lays out the question he seeks to address in this series of articles, namely "whether or not we shall try to win Socialism by means of political democracy, making use of the capitalist State machinery."

In the second part, Reed looks at the character of political democracy in America. He outlines the development of a capitalist elite in the United States, a process which he argues began in earnest during the American Civil War. He discusses the growth of the Progressive Movement led by Robert "Fighting Bob" La Follette and the initial achievements of the Wilson administration, which he contends came to power initially with the support of the small-property holder class. He argues, nevertheless, that Big Business interests hijacked these Progressive reforms and points to this as an example of the failure of political democracy. "The grand bourgeoisie," Reed writes, "makes use of the State to conserve and extend great capitalist interests at the expense of all other classes."

---

[8]Wolfe, *Strange Communists*, p. 35.

In his third installment, Jack Reed discusses labor unrest during World War I, then proceeds to outline the history of the labor movement in the United States, which he argues began with the American Civil War. "From before the Civil War to this day," he argues, "the psychology of the American worker has been the psychology not of a class-conscious laborer, but of a small property holder. The evolution of industrial society in America has been so swift that the American worker still has in his mind the idea that he may climb into the capitalist class... the American worker continues to believe the promises of the capitalist political parties, and *vote, vote, vote*." He goes on to discuss achievements of the Labor movement, such as the eight-hour workday, worker's compensation laws, restrictions on immigration, and others. He points that these achievements were superficial at best. He concludes that "Only after painful experience will Labor realize that the capitalist State is," quoting Karl Marx, "'nothing less than a machine for the oppression of one class by another, and that no less so in a democratic republic than under a monarchy.'"

In part four, Reed delves into the history of Socialism in the United States, tracing the origins of Socialist thought in the country and early Socialist movements up to the formation of the Workingman's Party of the United States in 1876. Throughout, he points to "the disastrous effect of political democratic ideology upon the growth of class-consciousness."

Reed continues his exposé on the history of Socialism in the United States in part five, discussing the establishment of the Socialist Labor Party and the subsequent struggles of the socialist movement to gain traction in the political system, and he recounts many incidents of violence against it. In Reed's eyes, "It is impossible to capture the capitalist state for the workers by means of the ballot; this has been demonstrated again and again; and yet when Labor repudiates political action, it is met with fearful violence." His analysis continues up to the founding of the Socialist Party of America in 1900. Despite its growth as a political movement in the preceding decades, in Reed's analysis, "the citadel of great capitalism is impregnable to all assaults except the mass assault of the united working class."

The sixth installment analyzes the Socialist Party of America. Reed asserts that the party was founded on "the prevailing American belief that the ballot controlled the State, and that the State could be conquered for the working class by the ballot." He discusses well-known Socialist leaders, such as Eugene V. Debs, Victor Berger, Meyer London, and others, mainly to show that none of them lived up to the ideals of Socialism. He argues that "nowhere in the world is the capitalist class so strongly organized and so firmly intrenched as in America..." and that because of this, "the American Socialist Party has shown a continuous tendency to draw away from the proletariat." In Reed's analysis, World War I clearly exposed the power of Capitalist political control.

Having concluded his analysis of Socialist political movements in the country, Jack Reed next focuses on why he believes that political democracy fails to ensure government by the majority. In this seventh segment of *Why Political Democracy Must Go*, he looks at the development of the American political system, which he says was "was designed by its founders to protect the rich against the poor, property against the necessities of life and liberty, and the monopolistic minority against the majority." He discusses the distrust of the centralized state by many of the founders of American independence, pointing to the Declaration of Independence as the embodiment of the ideal of the Middle Class who represented that movement. But Reed sees a profound shift early on in the new republic when the Constitution replaced the Articles of Confederation, ushering in a stronger central government designed to protect the interests of the wealthy elites. Reed interestingly points out that "The majority of the signers of the Declaration of Independence were Revolutionary leaders, men representing the small property holders; while the majority of the framers of the Constitution were the bankers, speculators in the land and money, and the merchants. Many delegates to the Constitutional Convention who had signed the Declaration of Independence refused to sign the Constitution, denouncing it as a "conspiracy"; among these was Benjamin Franklin."

Despite political reforms and amendments to the Constitution to make the political system seemingly more democratic, Reed points out that this is "only in proportion as the great capitalists strengthen the Invisible Government, and as the processes of "political democracy" became less and less able to overthrow their absolute hegemony – in other words, the center of Government has finally shifted completely from the Capitol and the White House to Wall Street." One hundred years later, many continue to echo these same sentiments.

In the eighth and final installment of *Why Political Democracy Must Go*, Jack Reed discusses the means by which the American capitalist class preserves and strengthens its power. He argues that the system of checks and balances enshrined in the Constitution thwarts the will of the people. Notably, he condemns the "autocracy of finance – which progressively nullifies the power of the political ballot." A century later, the influence of big money in American politics remains of major concern. He decries how "the Supreme Court has extended its powers of "interpretation" until it has become, in fact, a legislative body in itself." This refrain also continues to be heard a century later.

Reed's insights into how large capital exerts influence in American politics are as valid today as when he first penned them to paper. During a time when large capitalist interests have used their power to control the political system amidst the pandemic, the government has handed more and more power to large corporations to the detriment of small businesses and the American worker. Reed complains that the ruling elites ignore the Constitution and the laws when it suits their interests, and enforce them when it is politically expedient. He decried the censorship of his day, much the same as freedom-loving people decry it today.

Finally, Reed touches on the role of the press. Once again, his analysis remains valid when looking at the American media today: "The control of newspapers, and especially of the popular magazines, has of late years been concentrated in the hands of the great capitalistic interests, who are content even to lose money so long as they control the avenues of public expression." He adds that "Editors and reporters who do not conform to this view are discharged and boycotted; a black-list exists." Examples of this abound today when some of the country's wealthiest corporations and individuals own major newspapers and media outlets.

Reed concludes that political democracy is an illusion and that "The only power which the capitalist power cannot oppose is the organized and unified action of the proletarian mass."

***

John Reed remains one of the key figures in the history of the American left. His legend grew so that in the 1930s, John Reed clubs existed across the country. Several books have been written about him, and his life was the subject of a major motion picture, *Reds*, starring Warren Beatty and Diane Keaton.

Given his importance as a symbol of the American left, it is interesting to speculate about how Jack Reed might think about some of the major political issues of our day. While some may point to the progress made in the United States since he wrote at the end of World War I, Reed would continue to assert that "these "democratic" advances exactly correspond with the growth of the Invisible Government — the autocracy of finance — which progressively nullifies the power of the political ballot." He would find these forces are stronger today than when he decried them a century ago. Above all, John Reed would be appalled that large corporate interests have captured the left in America. He would equate today's tech tycoons with the oil and steel barons of his own time. He would see the nearly complete corporate control of the media and efforts at imposing censorship as anathema to the interests of the working class that he fought so hard to espouse.

Jack Reed would look at the focus on race and identity politics as yet another tool of capitalist oppression of the working class. He believed that the goal of large-scale capitalists is always to divide the working classes and distract their attention from economic questions. He would see efforts to allow mass immigration as another capitalist tool to suppress the wages of workers and strengthen the power of the capitalist elites against small property owners and the working class. He would see talk of "Democratic Socialism," much the same as he saw it a hundred years ago, as an illusion, and he would point to a plethora of examples of how the Capitalist elites have co-opted the movement to serve their own interests.

A century after writing *Why Political Democracy Must Go*, Jack Reed would still see the American worker duped by "the illusion of the ballot-box," and blinded by the false promises of political democracy. I think it fair to say that Reed would be a fierce opponent of political correctness and censorship as oppressive to the human spirit. His close friend Max Eastman summed it up best, writing, "He was my friend, long loved and admired, and his enduring loyalty as I felt it was that of an individualist to his vision of truth, and of a poet to the free and full experience of life. He was very American, and would have a hard time learning the alien trick of identifying liberty, or the receding hope of it, with obedience to the heads of a tightly centralized and disciplined organization."[9] Above all, John Reed was a man of principle. Much as he died disillusioned with the Bolshevik Regime in the Soviet Union, he would be distraught at the twenty-first-century alliance between the American Left, the Tech monopolies, and Wall Street tycoons.

---

[9] Max Eastman, *Love and Revolution: My Journey Through an Epoch* (New York: Random House, 1964), p. 260.

Amid the pandemic, it is worthwhile to consider Reed's warning that "in abnormal times political democracy breaks down, and it is always abnormal times when the capitalist class fears that the workers may conquer political power."

He would see that we still live in very dangerous times and that the threat to the working class of America looms as large as ever. Jack Reed would continue to decry the illusion of political democracy and fight to make the working class understand that "political democracy" will never serve to defend their interests.

A.K. Brackob

MODERATE "Socialism" — Menshevism — Right Wingism — is based largely on the theory that the class struggle will be won by capturing the political power through the ballot box — that through a process of gradual, orderly progress, the election of candidates to office and the passage of social reform legislation, capitalism will grow weaker and weaker, and the Constitution will be amended into a charter of the Cooperative Commonwealth, or be peaceably abolished.

The modern capitalist state, in the words of Marx, is

nothing less than a machine for the oppression of one class by another, and that not less so in a democratic republic than under a monarchy.

This proposition was the rock upon which the Second International split at the beginning of the European war. The dominant moderate "Socialists" of all countries sooner or later embraced the formula that "political democracy is better than autocracy." In Germany, the majority Social Democratic leaders told their followers, "*Russia threatens 'free' Germany. We must mobilize against Tsarism.*" In France,

England, and Italy, they said *"Defend Democracy against autocracy. German militarism threatens us. This is the war that will end war."*

The class-conscious proletariat of all lands was ripe for mass opposition to the War. The workers knew instinctively that this War had nothing whatever to do with "democracy" or "autocracy" — but was merely an intense form of competition between two groups of world-grasping imperialistic Powers, struggling for control of markets which had been made necessary through the gigantic development of Finance-Imperialism.

Especially in America was this fact clear. Not by the remotest stretch of the Rooseveltian imagination could the people be convinced that we were threatened by any "autocracy" — except industrial autocracy, which had already captured the country. The United States declared war after three years of European conflict had brought home to the understanding of the class-conscious workers of neutral countries, with sickening clearness, the falsity of the Wilsonian formula, "To make the world safe for democracy."

In entering the War, the ruling class of the United States played the part of a banker who has heavily financed one of the two huge competing trusts, and who, to defend his investment, must throw in all his resources to get rid of the competitor.

Hence the St. Louis Resolution of the American Socialist Party — the mandate of the rank and file of the Party to the Party leaders, which was disregarded by them again and again as they surrendered, little by little, their opposition to the War.[10]

The formation of the Left Wing, and its sharp call to the Socialist movement to abolish the social reform-planks in Party platforms, has posed with cutting distinctness the question of whether or not we shall try to win Socialism by means of political democracy, making use of the capitalist State machinery.

---

[10]A resolution adopted at the National Emergency Convention of the Socialist Party of the United States held in St. Louis from April 7-14, 1917, and ratified by referendum of the membership. It declared that "The Socialist Party of the United States in the present grave crisis solemnly reaffirms it allegiance to the principle of internationalism and working class solidarity the world over, and proclaims its unalterable opposition to the war just declared by the government of the United States." Party leaders later disregarded the resolution. (A.K.B.)

II

Let us for the moment examine the character of American political democracy.

In this country, as in all modern "democratic" countries, there are two sides to government — political and economic. The policies of modern "democratic" countries are dictated by the capitalist "interests." As Woodrow Wilson has pointed out in his *New Freedom*, the government of this country is in the hands of the great aggregations of capital.[11]

This process of concentration of wealth into the hands of the few began during the Civil War, when the manufacturers of munitions of war, the purveyors of provisions, and the speculators piled up colossal fortunes. This was the period when J.P. Morgan laid the foundations of his riches by selling defective rifles to the Government, and John Wanamaker by providing shoddy uniforms for the Union troops. The floating of Government War Loans, also, brought into the hands of a few bankers an immense financial power. Immediately after the War, the looting of

---

[11]Woodrow Wilson, *The New Freedom* (New York: Doubleday, 1914). (A.K.B.)

the South, the expansion of industry, the girdling of the continent with railroads, the spoliation of natural resources, and the speculation in land, assumed vast proportions, and became glaringly apparent to the petit bourgeoisie — the small property holders.

This class then consisted largely of farmers. The rest of the population, when hard-pressed, could always leave the cities and go out on the measureless free lands of the West. So, the first revolt of the small property holders was against land-looting, and culminated with partial success in the Homestead Law.[12]

But the farmer was at the mercy of all the great interests. They controlled the railroads, the markets, the banks, the price of tools. In spite of the high prices paid for produce during the War, the farmer was badly in debt. *He* had not been able to purchase Government securities, but he had been forced to pay ruinous taxes, whose imposition was supported by the manufacturers in the towns, because they *actually stimulated business.*

---

[12]Enacted in 1862, the Homestead Act provided that any adult citizen, or intended citizen, who had never borne arms against the U.S. government could claim 160 acres of surveyed government land. Claimants had to improve the land either by building a dwelling or cultivating it. After 5 years, the original filer was entitled to the property, free and clear, except for a small registration fee. (A.K.B.)

The new money-kings were manipulating the currency so that the Government would redeem the depreciated securities held by them, and throw the burden on the backs of the workers and the small property holders. This led to the beginnings of revolt against the great interests, in which the foundation was Cheap Money — Greenbackism, Populism, and later, Bryan's Free Silver campaigns of twenty-five years ago.[13]

This is the *real* American ancestry of American Socialism, upon which were grafted the theories of Marxian and — predominantly — Lasallean Socialism brought from Europe by the Germans who emigrated after 1848; and the Fourierism introduced by Albert Brisbane and Horace Greeley.[14]

---

[13]William Jennings Bryan (1860-1925) of Nebraska ran unsuccessfully for president as the candidate of the Democratic Party in 1896, 1900, and 1908. He served as Secretary of State under Woodrow Wilson from 1913 to 1915. Bryan favored using silver to back the dollar at a value that would inflate the prices farmers received for their crops, easing their debt burden, as opposed to strict adherence to the more carefully fixed money supply implicit in the gold standard. His position became known as the Free Silver Movement. (A.K.B.)

[14]*Fourierism* was a set of economic, political, and social beliefs first espoused by the French intellectual Charles Fourier (1772–1837). He envisioned a utopian form of socialism involving communal associations of people who worked and lived together as part of the human future. (A.K.B.)

The next revolt of the petit bourgeoisie in America was the Progressive Movement. This also occurred after a war — in this case a frankly Imperialistic war which marked the formal entrance of American capitalism into the period of Capitalist Imperialism. The whole period was summed up in the emergence of the great trusts during the administration of McKinley and Mark Hanna, the open advocacy of high tariffs, no longer to "protect infant industries," or to increase wages, but as a basis for the great monopolies of the means of production and distribution in the United States, and a weapon in the international war of Capitalist Imperialism — "Dollar Diplomacy."[15]

The Progressive Movement properly so-called, was a reform movement to reshape the Republican Party so that it would not be smashed by the growing hostility of the small property-holders, made desperate by the ruthlessness of Big Business. It advocated all sorts of checks upon the power of Big Business — reform of the electoral laws, so as to give the small property-holders a voice in the government (initiative and referendum, recall, direct election of Senators, Woman

---

[15]Dollar diplomacy was the foreign policy adopted by President William Howard Taft and his Secretary of State Philander C. Knox to minimize the use or threat of military force and instead further United States interests in Latin America and East Asia through the use of economic power, guaranteeing loans made to foreign countries. (A.K.B.)

Suffrage); low tariff (a sort of modified Free Trade); and many other measures of relief, which were expressed with all their significance and all their short-sightedness in the various Anti-Trust Acts, Interstate Commerce Commissions, etc.

La Follette[16] was the strongest and most uncompromising leader of the Progressive Movement; he awakened, first, the small property-holders of his State, and then of the entire country. The great capitalists who at first fought Progressivism, finally realized the futility of open battle, and resorted to their time-honored tactics of capturing the movement. Men like George Perkins, of the United States Steel Corporation — one of the most powerful of the trusts — financed the Progressive Party and became one of its leaders. To speak plainly, he bought it. Roosevelt, when in the White House, at first fought the Progressives. Being a shrewd politician, however, he soon saw that Progressivism was going to win, and took over most of the weapons in the Progressive armory, flourishing them aloft in the sight of all men, and emitting loud cries. The fight of

---

[16]Robert M. "Fighting Bob" La Follette (1855-1925) is the most famous figure in Wisconsin political history. He served as Governor and represented the state in both houses of Congress as a member of the Republican Party. A leader of the progressive movement in the early twentieth century, La Follette ran for President in 1924 as the nominee of the Progressive Party, garnering over 16% of the vote. (A.K.B.)

Progressivism against the trusts assumed such proportions that it blocked the Morgan interests in their plans for consolidating the steel industry of the country in one huge, profitable and invincible trust. Whereupon, the Morgan interests unleashed the panic of 1907, and the Government gave in.

This was not the end, however. The Movement under La Follette assumed great proportions. More and more openly, with an ever greater and greater following, La Follette attacked Big Business. The plutocracy was frightened. Its agents, Perkins and others, attempted in vain to check the growth of petit bourgeois revolt. Roosevelt, returning from Africa, was making a triumphal tour of Europe, among other things reviewing the Prussian Guard at the side of the Kaiser. Emissaries of Perkins went to meet him, and secret plans were laid by which La Follette was to be displaced.

The opportunity arrived. La Follette, Progressivism's Presidential candidate, was invited to the Publishers' Dinner in Philadelphia. There, with characteristic frankness, he told the editors and publishers of America that "*the press was controlled by Big Business which used it to exterminate the petit bourgeoisie.*"[17]

---

[17]Although the press, especially the monthly magazines, had for years carried on the battle of Progressivism — the period of "mucking-racking" — by this time (1912), it had been pretty generally taken over by the great financial interests, and had ceased

This was the signal for Big Business to attack. The artillery of the great press, which had been conciliating its subscribers — the majority of whom were small property holders — by commenting favorably upon Progressivism, now turned upon La Follette and blasted him with contempt and ridicule. And at the same time, Perkins and the other leaders came out for Roosevelt as the Progressive candidate.

The Republican Party, willing to lose rather than to adopt the La Follettism with which the rank and file of the petit bourgeoisie was infected, insolently suppressed the small property-holders in the Chicago Convention in 1912.[18] The Progressives made a fight, but it was a losing fight, and they knew it, and so did the small property-holders all over the country, who, despairing of the Republican Party, threw most of their support to the Democrats.

Big Business knew that the small property-holders would probably elect the President and Congress, but they

---

its attacks on vested interests. I shall treat this question in a later installment. (J.R.)

[18]The battle for the presidential nomination at Republican Party convention in 1912 pitted incumbent President William Howard Taft against former President Theodore Roosevelt and Wisconsin Senator Robert M. La Follette. Although Taft was nominated for a second-term, the Progressive-wing split from the party and nominated Roosevelt on a third-party ticket. La Follette, however, refused to support Roosevelt. This split in the party led to the election of Democrat Woodrow Wilson. (A.K.B.)

also realized that the great trusts were so firmly intrenched in power that they could not be dislodged. Also, the "interests" would be in the position of Opposition Party, where they could safely sabotage the Democratic administration and at the same time criticize it for being inefficient.

Woodrow Wilson, author of the *New Freedom,* was elected to the Presidency by the small property-holders — the Progressive elements. The achievements of his first administration reflect the constituency which elected him.

First, *defeat of the open Imperialist scheme to annex Mexico.* The small property-holder is not a partner in Imperialism, any more than he is a partner in the great trusts. Capitalist Imperialism does away with the small property-holder. Therefore, he is opposed to annexations, and can afford to give his humanitarian sentiments full play.

Second, *the Federal Reserve Act.* The small property-holder has a desperate fear of financial panics, which eliminate him at one blow. He wants to guard against them, and stabilize finance so that the plutocrats cannot destroy him at will.

Third, *Taxation of Great Wealth.* The Income and Inheritance taxes are for the purpose of relieving the overwhelming burden of taxation which lies upon the small property-holder.

Fourth, *The Industrial Relations Commission, Child Labor Law, etc.* Social legislation is the small property-holder's method of reforming capitalism so that he can exist in it. He is at the mercy of both organized Labor and organized Capital, and is more affected by labor troubles than the great capitalist. He must conciliate both Labor and Capital. At the same time, he is not interested in wholesale cheap labor, and he himself is too close to the proletariat, and too liable to be pushed into its ranks, to relish the idea of mass starvation and debauchery of the workers.

In 1912 and 1913, the abuses of savage industrial tyranny provoked a series of gigantic labor troubles — Lawrence, Paterson, Michigan, Colorado, etc. The small property-holder became alarmed, and demanded that these abuses be remedied.

So much for the most important political victories of what were, without contradiction, the great majority of the voters in the United States — the small property-holders and those dominated by their psychology.[19] If political "democracy" worked, this majority, which elected the President, and swept Congress and the Legislatures, should have been able to enforce its will.

But what has actually happened? The Imperialist scheme to annex Mexico was temporarily defeated — *but last*

---

[19]The Eight-hour Law belongs to a category which I shall treat later. (J.R.)

month the American State Department warned the Mexican Government not to dare carry out its plan of heavily taxing the oil-wells owned by American capitalists — and passports were given to American oil-kings to go to Paris and present their private-property claims to the Peace Conference. And even as I write, a counter-revolution financed by American and foreign oil-interests, with a bureau of information in New York's financial district, is attempting to overthrow the Carranza Government, and promising in case of success to leave the property of foreigners alone.

During the War, the United States Government, with armed force, has overthrown the Governments of two Caribbean countries, Haiti and Santa Domingo, and set up a military dictatorship there.

The Federal Reserve Act, designed to avoid panics, was framed by the Big Interests. It does not provide against panics — but on the contrary, it places the Treasury of the United States at the mercy of the great financial interests.

Great wealth has been taxed to run the Government, and the War — but the Government has become more and more an instrument designed to protect and foster private property; that is to say, to create ever more and more great wealth.

The Industrial Relations Commission discovered such hideous industrial conditions in America, conditions which pointed so definitely to the fact that only the Social Revolution could cure them, that the small property-holders became frightened. The Commission was discredited by both plutocratic and Progressive press (such papers as *The New Republic* being particularly exasperated by the "intemperateness" of its report). Nothing ever came of it, except such schemes as John D. Rockefeller's, which pretended to cure conditions by making Labor even more helpless.

The Child Labor Law was declared "unconstitutional" by the Supreme Court, in spite of the widely-heralded appointment of Louis D. Brandeis, a Liberal, as Supreme Court Justice.

Thus, we can see the failure of political democracy even among the ruling class — the property-holders, where Marx says one of its most important functions is to act as arbitrator.

The grand bourgeoisie makes use of the State to conserve and extend great capitalist interests at the expense of all other classes.

During the War, the American Labor Unions were attacked under the pretense of "military necessity," their union regulations broken down, and results of years of organization wiped out. Pleading "patriotism," the employers' associations represented in the Council of National Defense and other bodies secured the suspension of labor legislation in some states. Men who were persistently active in labor organization, or who failed to buy Liberty bonds or contribute to the Red Cross, were thrown out of work, and rendered liable to the Army draft. Whole striking factories were threatened with instant conscription into the Army. In some parts of the country such workers, not only for opposing the war, but even for opposing the ruthless profiteering of employers, were blacklisted by the Councils of National Defense. At the same time, private police and detective organizations, composed of business men and manufacturers, and authorized by the Department of Justice, used their power to crush labor organization wherever possible.

The Government created a joint body of workers' and employers' representatives called the War Labor Board, to settle industrial disputes. In many cases the awards, presumably binding upon the employers, were either accepted and not applied, or else partially disregarded. The most powerful corporations, such as the United States Steel Corporation, which has always resisted with terrorism and brute force all attempts of its employees at organization, the War Labor Board did not dare openly to affront.

Protests of the workers against unfair awards of arbitrators during the War were met by defiance and threats from Government officials — such as the flat refusal of Charles Piez, Director of the Emergency Fleet Corporation, to reconsider the Macy award to the Shipyard Workers of Seattle, and his ferocious denunciations of the men.[20]

These measures proceeded from an Administration which Organized Labor had united almost solidly to elect, and whose leader — President Wilson — had flattered the vanity of the workers by reviewing the Labor Day parade with Samuel Gompers in 1916; and during a War which Organized Labor in America had voted overwhelmingly to support in the name of democracy....

---

[20]In November 1918 the Shipbuilding Labor Adjustment Board issued a ruling — known as the Macy Award after its chairman, V. Everit Macy (1871-1930), setting wages for skilled and unskilled workers in shipyards across the country. The ruling had a side effect of reducing wages for some workers and led to a massive strike of shipyard workers in Seattle at the beginning of 1919. (A.K.B.)

A typical sufferer during the War was the Machinists' Union. The employers discovered that a skilled, highly-paid machinist was a useless luxury. Four unskilled workers could be taught each one part of a machinist's job, in a very short time. These four comparatively unskilled workers could do the work of four machinists, and do it much cheaper, thus destroying the union wage-scale, and throwing the skilled workers on the street.

It is interesting in this connection to quote from an article in *Fincher's Trades' Review*, written by William H. Sylvis,[21] the first great American labor leader, in 1863, describing the same process applied to the Stove-Moulders:

> "Simultaneous with this was introduced the 'helper system'.... the stoves were cut up, that is, each man made one piece.... Thus, this system went on until it became necessary for each man to have from one to five boys; and... prices became so low that men were obliged to increase the hours of labor, and work much harder; and then could scarcely obtain the plainest necessities of life..."

It was directly from these conditions that the first powerful national labor union sprang — the Molders' International Union. Likewise, it was the replacing of skilled

---

[21]William H. Sylvis (1828–1869) founded the National Labor Union, union federation in the United States that attempted to unite workers from various crafts into a single national organization. (A.K.B.)

men with young apprentice-boys, at starvation wages, which was the chief grievance resulting in the second great union — the National Union of Machinists and Blacksmiths, under the leadership of another of the famous early American labor leaders, Jonathan C. Fincher.[22]

The beginning of the Civil War,[23] with its industrial paralysis and widespread unemployment, wiped out whatever tentative labor organization had begun, except for the two great national unions above mentioned. But in 1862 the Government began its issuance of hundreds of millions of dollars in "greenbacks," which, accompanied by the high war tariff and the tremendous demand for army supplies, caused a hectic revival of industry, and laid the foundations for a class of capitalist employers. As in the European War just concluded, all classes profited except the wage-earners; for while wages in 1864 had risen 30%, the average of retail prices had risen 70%.

---

[22]Jonathan C. Fincher was head of the Machinists and Blacksmiths Union and worked with William H. Sylvis to establish the National Labor Union in 1866. (A.K.B.)

[23]Mass meetings of workingmen to protest against the Civil War were held in Philadelphia, Reading, Norfolk, Peterborough and Richmond, Va., Cincinnati, St. Louis and Louisville, Ky., at which latter place a resolution was adopted declaring that "workingmen had no real or vital issue in the mere abstract questions used to divide the masses." A national convention of workers met in Philadelphia in 1861 to oppose the War. (J.R.)

The frightful pressure on the working-class at this time led to an era of labor union organization, most of the unions being local, and affiliated in trades assemblies, which supported one another in strikes and boycotts. The local and scattered character of these small unions corresponded exactly to the conditions of production at the time. But by the end of the war the manufacture of standardized products, and the establishment, through the new railroads, of national markets, created rapidly, one after another, the great national unions. This was the real birth of the American Labor Movement.

Before the Civil War, the Government was controlled by the Southern slave-holding class. This control was challenged by the small capitalists of the North, opposing the interests of wage labor to those of chattel-slavery. It was as a representative of this small property-holding class that Abraham Lincoln was elected to the Presidency, and as a representative of this class that he conducted the war. He feared the growing ruthless power of Wall Street, and warned against it again and again. And when the war was ended, with the slave-power destroyed, he wished to see Reconstruction in the South proceed rapidly and generously, so that the rising class of small property-holders there could unite with the same class in the North to keep control of the Government. But Lincoln was assassinated, and there is no small evidence to prove that the bullet which killed him was fired from the direction of Wall Street....[24] And the capitalists, seizing control of the Federal Government, proceeded to loot the South, and to create there such bitter sectional and racial antagonism, that it made cooperation between the small property holders of the North and South impossible and enabled a small group of capitalists to settle themselves firmly in the saddle. Finally, abandoning the ruined South, the ruling class turned its attention to looting the public domain, natural resources, and the Government — State and National. Great political machines were built up throughout the country, resting on political patronage and Governmental graft, whose power to this day has never been shaken off.

Before the Civil War, there were no great capitalists. Industry was largely localized; the products being consumed where they were manufactured. There was plenty of free land in the West to which the exploited could go, and the workman could always become a small manufacturer and merchant on his own account. Literally speaking, *there was no wage-earning working-class as such in the United States.* But the free workingmen of America who enlisted or were drafted into the Union armies, leaving a

---

[24]There is a conspiracy theory around the assassination of President Abraham Lincoln by John Wilkes Booth that a group of powerful Bankers, financiers, businessmen, cotton speculators, and profiteers encouraged and financed the assassination. (A.K.B.)

society in which the manufacturer came to them, returned after the war to find gigantic new centralized industries, to which they must travel and beg for work. With the development of power, transportation and great factories, industry after industry left the country and moved to the city; and the worker was forced to follow. This concentration in the cities was intensified by the waves of immigration from Europe. Free land was gone; not even the Homestead Law, breaking up the great land-holdings and creating millions of small land-owners, could prevent the growing concentration of labor power and capital. In fact, the new free-holders were at the mercy of the railroads, marketing facilities, and banks, which were already in the hands of the great capitalists.

From before the Civil War to this day, the psychology of the American worker has been the psychology not of a class-conscious laborer, but of a small property holder. The evolution of industrial society in America has been so swift, that the American worker still has in his mind the idea that he may climb into the capitalist class.

Why?

Not the least of the reasons is, that two or three generations before Labor in other countries had received the first privilege for which it fought, the American worker had been given *the political vote*. The first manifestations of his class consciousness were *political* manifestations. In spite of unending disappointments, in spite of the hollowness of all his legislative victories, the American worker continues to believe the promises of the capitalist political parties, and *vote, vote, vote.*

It is to be noticed that the beginnings of American economic labor organization were dictated by the necessity for *defense* of his class interests — never *offense.* The Knights of Labor was founded to *defend* standards of living; the American Federation of Labor was formed to *defend* Labor's interests. Except comparatively lately, as partially in the I.W.W.,[25] American Labor has never supported any economic organization with a *political* object — that is to say, with the object of gaining control of the State. Its efforts at political conquest of government have been in the form of political action — and this political action has never been a class-conscious proletarian movement, but always the joining of forces with the small property holders, in *their* efforts to conquer power. Such was the Union Labor Party, the Greenback Labor Party, the Populists, the Bryan Free-Silverites, the Progressives, and finally the Wilson Democrats. And, as we have noted in a preceding installment, these movements, which in essence were

---

[25]Founded in Chicago in 1905, the Industrial Workers of the World, or I.W.W., was a general union with the goal of uniting all workers into "One Big Union." Closely aligned with socialist goals, it supported the overthrow of capitalism and the establishment of industrial democracy. One of its most prominent leaders during this period was William "Big Bill" Haywood (1869-1928). (A.K.B.)

nothing more than revolts of debtors against the strangling greed of the great capitalists, failed utterly. The control of Government by the great capitalists was too strong to break.

In all these debtor-revolts, the farmer, who feels the pressure the most severely, was the most prominent element. Union labor followed the farmer — not as the propertyless industrial worker, but as the owner, or prospective owner, of a little property. The latest of these revolutionary movements of small property holders is the Non-Partisan League, with its program of State banks, State-controlled elevators and transportation lines, and its combination of the farmer with Union Labor in the cities to wrest control of the State from the great financial interests. It, too, will fail....[26]

For more than half a century, American Labor has turned its attention alternately from politics to economic organization. Says John R. Commons, in his *History of American Labor*:[27]

The repeating cycle of politics and trade unionism, political struggle and economic struggle, political

---

[26]Founded in 1915 by former Socialist leader Arthur C. Townley, the Non-Partisan League, as Reed predicted, ultimately failed. By 1950, it had merged with the Democratic Party. (A.K.B.)

[27]Commons, John R., et al. *History of Labor in the United States*. Vols. 1–4 (New York: Macmillan, 1918–1935). (A.K.B.)

organization and economic organization, marks out the course of this history of labor.

In the last two decades before the European War, Union Labor, disenchanted with the failure of political action, adopted the course of adjuring politics, and developing the economic organization alone.

In the last decade before the European War, the Employer's Association had captured both Houses of Congress, and was using the Courts to revive "conspiracy" charges against labor organizations, and to defeat them by means of the injunction, turned its attention to politics in order to protect its economic action. Political pressure was brought to bear upon legislatures; lobbies were maintained at Washington and in the State legislatures; the policy of "voting for our friends and defeating our enemies" was largely practiced; Mr. Samuel Gompers[28] and other labor leaders were familiar figures in Congressional Committee rooms, arguing for or against such and such a bill.

The legislative achievements of Union Labor are impressive. A Department of Labor in Washington, and State bureaus in almost every State; eight-hour laws in

---

[28]A cigar-maker by trade, Samuel Gompers (1850-1924) was a key figure in American labor history. He founded the American Federation of Labor (A.F. of L.), and served as its president from 1886 to 1894, and again from 1895 until his death in 1924. (A.K.B.)

Government work, on the railways, and in many States; Federal Boards of Arbitration and Conciliation; Workmen's Compensation laws in most States; restriction of foreign immigration, and exclusion of Oriental laborers; Factory laws of all sorts, legislative safeguards, and legalization of strikes and picketing; and the Clayton Act, which declares that Labor is not a commodity, and professes to abolish the use of injunctions in industrial disputes — a law which Mr. Gompers hailed as "the new Magna Charta."[29]

But in the last analysis, what does all this come down to? The Department of Labor in Washington represents nothing but the interests of the upper strata of skilled workers; it is headed by a former workingman, William B. Wilson, who acquiesces in the persecutions of striking miners by the copper barons of Arizona, and defends the deportation from the country of foreigners active in labor organization, on the ground that they are "Bolshevik!"; in other words, it faithfully serves the capitalist Government. Long before the Eight-Hour laws were enacted, it was recognized by the more intelligent capitalist-employers that they would increase the efficiency of workmen; and even now they are not obeyed by corporations whose interests they do not serve. Boards of Arbitration either "arbitrate" in favor of the employers, who will not relinquish an atom of

---

[29]Enacted in 1914, the Clayton Act was an important piece of anti-trust legislation that sought to stop anti-competitive practices. (A.K.B.)

their power, or fail. Most Workmen's Compensation laws are subject to decisions of Industrial Commissions, or similar Government bodies, and to appeal in the capitalist courts. Factory laws are generally disregarded, and strikes and picketing, though legalized, are still practically outlawed by the police. The Clayton Act is not worth the paper it is printed on.

In spite of the phenomenal growth of the American Federation of Labor, and its increase of power, nevertheless industry has grown faster yet. Even before the war, that great achievement of the American Federation of Labor, the "trade agreement," a sort of partnership between organized labor and capital, — in which contracts were signed between bargaining groups to cover a period of time — had been abolished in the largest companies, such as the United States Steel Corporation. Little by little, the "basic" industries are lost to Organized Labor. And the great mass of the unskilled workers, deliberately excluded from the ranks of the privileged skill workers of the Federation, had been recruited by the I.W.W., which abjured political action of any sort, and whose object was the conquest of the State by economic action.

The end of the European War leaves the great capitalists in command of the industrial world, and determined, if they can, to destroy labor organization for good and all.

This is the result of the votes of the workers who put the Democratic Administration in power.

To meet this menace a powerful movement has sprung up in the ranks of Union Labor, to form a Labor Party — a political organization which, by means of legislative reforms, will conquer power for the workers. Its program bears the marks of its historical genealogy — the psychology of the small property holder, and not of the proletarian.

The method of its organization shows once more American Labor's invincible trust in the vote, and in the possibility of "partnership" with the capitalist class.

Only after painful experience will Labor realize that the capitalist State is *"nothing less than a machine for the oppression of one class by another, and that no less so in a democratic republic than under a monarchy."*

Labor cannot enter into "partnership" within the capitalist State. Labor can only win the product of its toil by the overthrow of the entire capitalist system — nothing less.

¥ V

The history of Socialism in America is of the most absorbing interest. Every new theory of cohorts for a descent upon the 3d, 5th rings of the factory system, had its immediate repercussion in the New World. The present Left Wing movement in the Socialist Party, with its reflex of the new tendencies of European Socialism, is, in that characteristic, not exceptional.

For example, in 1826, the Englishman, Robert Owen, moved to America and started his New Harmony colony. About the same time, Albert Brisbane (father of Arthur Brisbane, Mr. Hearst's right-hand man), introduced into America the philosophy of Fourier, to which he converted Horace Greeley; this resulted in a series of communistic experiments in cooperative industry and agriculture. Greeley abandoned pure Fourierism, and tinkered with "profit- sharing" and other varieties of cooperation, that led to the great movement for producers' and consumers' cooperatives in New England, which culminated and then died down in the eighties.

The characteristic of native American social ideas was their intense individualism. The economic reason for this was, the historical condition of American social development, which identified the concentration of labor, and capital in cities with the loss of individual liberty characteristic of a population largely agricultural and scattered thinly over a great area.

One of the earliest native social philosophies was transcendentalism, which took various forms, including the esthetic individualism of Thoreau; the intellectual individualism of Emerson — whose ideas, however, were considered so dangerous to society that he was not permitted to lecture at Harvard University;[30] the "associationist" cooperative activity of Channing, grafted onto Fourierism; and finally, the revolutionary ideas of Orestes Brownson.[31]

---

[30]Ralph Waldo Emerson (1803-1882) was one of the key figures of the transcendentalist movement in the United States. After delivering an address at the Harvard Divinity School in 1838, in which he declared that Jesus was a great man, but not God, he was shunned as an atheist and would not return to speak at Harvard for another 30 years. (A.K.B.)

[31]Orestes Brownson (1803-1876) was an intellectual, preacher, and labor activist, active in the Transcendentalist movement. In his book, *New Views of Christianity, Society, and the Church,* he combined Transcendentalist religious views with radical social egalitarianism, sharply criticizing the unequal social distribution of wealth as un-Christian and unprincipled. He later converted to Catholicism and renounced these ideas. (A.K.B.)

Brownson, of the above, was the only real member of the working class. It is interesting here to quote from his article, "The Laboring Classes," published in 1840, an account of the factories of New England, where the workers were mostly women:

> The great mass wear out their health, spirits and morals without becoming one whit better off than when they commenced labor. The bills of mortality in these villages are not striking, we admit, for the poor girls when they can toil no longer go home to die. We know no sadder sight on earth than one of our factory villages presents when the bell at break of day, or at the hour of breakfast or dinner, calls out its hundreds or thousands of operatives.

Read this, and then go to Lawrence, or Providence, or Fall River today. The only difference is that now the workers are foreign women, while then they were Americans.

Brownson had never seen the *Communist Manifesto*. Yet, in 1840, he advocated the overthrow of the capitalist state, and declared any means justifiable. It is startling at this time to read what he says:

> And is this measure to be easily carried? Not at all. It will cost infinitely more than it cost to abolish either hereditary monarchy or hereditary nobility. It is a great measure and a startling. The rich, the business community, will never voluntarily consent to it, and we think we know too much of human nature to believe that it will ever be effected peaceably. It will be effected only by the strong arm of physical force. *It will come, if it ever*

comes at all, only at the conclusion of a war, the like of which the world has yet never witnessed, and from which, however inevitable it may seem to the eye of philosophy, the heart of humanity recoils with horror.

We are not ready for this measure yet. There is much previous work to be done, and we should be the last to bring it before the legislature. The time, however, has come for its free and full discussion. It must be canvassed in the public mind, and society prepared for acting on it.

Another direction taken by native American social theories was reform of the systems of exchange and banking.

Josiah Warren,[32] the "first American anarchist," opened a series of stores where goods were sold at cost, and the labor of the salesmen was paid for by an equal amount of labor by the purchaser. He founded several colonies, which were based on the principle that price should be determined by labor-cost. He was followed by William Beck, with his "ticket-system" of doing away with banks, and the substitution of purchasing power for currency. Then came William Weitling, the German immigrant, with his plan for a "bank of exchange," in which price would be fixed by "labor-time." This was a compromise with the ideas which he had first brought from Europe in 1847 — *common ownership of all property and centralized management of*

---

[32]Josiah Warren (1798-1874) is widely regarded as the first American anarchist. His ideas centered around Mutualism, which advocated a socialist society based on free markets. (A.K.B.)

production and exchange. The reason for this change is very significant. Both in Europe and America the merchant-capitalist was the dominant enemy of the working class. But in Europe it was realized that a social and political revolution was necessary to get rid of him (indicated by the Revolutions of 1848), while in America, the workers demanded *economic reforms which would not destroy existing political institutions.*

The first appearance in this country of Marxian Socialism was in 1852-3, when Joseph Weydemeyer,[33] a friend and disciple of Marx and Engels, came to New York and organized a short-lived revolutionary society known as the *Proletarierbund.* Then he attempted to spread his ideas in the ranks of the trade unions forming at the time, and organized an association among the German workers called the General Workingmen's Alliance, which began the publication of a Communist paper called *Die Reform.* The movement spread. A similar organization was started among the English-speaking workers. But the growing wave of trade-unionism finally overwhelmed it, and Marxian Socialism, with its conception of the class struggle, its

---

[33]Joseph Weydemeyer (1818-1866) was a prominent early American socialist. He was a friend of Marx and Engels, advocating for "Utopian socialism." He participated in the 1848 revolutions in Germany before immigrating to the United States in 1851. A staunch supporter of Abraham Lincoln, he served as a lieutenant colonel in the Union Army during the Civil War. (A.K.B.)

recognition of trade-unionism and political action, disappeared until after the Civil War .

The First International, founded in London in 1864, for which Karl Marx wrote the inaugural address, began with an organization of British trade union leaders to prevent the importation of strikebreakers into England from the continent. It developed into a sort of general Workers' Union, in whose ranks two theories battled; that of Mazzini,[34] advocating the harmony of the interests of capital and labor (from which the philosophy of the A.F. of L. is directly descended), and that of Marx, who emphasized the class solidarity of labor in all lands. Not until the Bakuninites[35] almost captured the movement in the early seventies did the actual program of Socialism become the leading issue. The early philosophy of the International was based on the economic organization of the workers into trade unions and cooperatives, to precede the seizure of the

---

[34]Giuseppe Mazzini (1805-1872) was a revolutionary leader and one of the architects of Italian unification. Although he entered a dialogue with socialists, he could not accept the Marxist concept of class struggle as the driving force in history. (A.K.B.)

[35]Mikhail Alexandrovich Bakunin (1814-1876) was a Russian socialist revolutionary and the founder of collectivist anarchism. He vehemently opposed Marxism, predicting that the dictatorship of the proletariat would transform into one party dictatorship over the proletariat. (A.K.B.)

political state. It took ten years for this idea to become firmly established in America.

On the other hand, the Lasallean agitation of 1863 in Germany was immediately reproduced here. Lasalle emphasized political action, the political capture of the State *first* — this capture to be followed by the organization of the working class into cooperatives assisted by State credit.

In 1865, there was formed in New York the General German Workingmen's Union, which subsequently became Section I of the International. Its original declared:

> Under the name of the General German Workingmen's Union are united all Social-Republicans, particularly those who regard Ferdinand Lasalle as the most eminent champion of the working class, for the purpose of reaching a true point of view on all social questions....
> *While in Europe only a general evolution can form the means of uplifting the working people, in America, the education of the masses will instill them with the degree of self-confidence that is indispensable for the effective and intelligent use of the ballot, and will eventually lead to the emancipation of the working people from the yoke of capital.*

Seven years before this, however, there had been established a Marxian organization, the Communist Club, based on the *Communist Manifesto*, among whom were many members afterward prominent in the American International, and who conducted a voluminous correspondence with Marx, Engels, and Becker.

In 1868, the Communist Club and the Workingmen's Union united to form a political party, the Social Party of New York and vicinity. It is interesting to note here that this party was, out of deference to the English-speaking workers, a distinctly social reform party, advocating progressive income taxes, abolition of national banks, right of issue of paper money reserved to the Government, an eight-hour law, etc. The campaign of 1868 proved it a failure. In December of 1869, it joined the International, and began work of Socialist study and general Socialist propaganda, on the basis of Marx's *Capital*.

In the next two years, a number of new sections of the International were organized, consisting mostly of foreign immigrants. There was a French section, a Bohemian section, and several Irish sections. But besides the foreign immigrants, there was another group, Americans, who joined the International. This was made up of intellectuals, inheritors of the traditions of transcendentalism and Fourierism in the forties and fifties. They had formed an organization called the New Democracy, whose platform advocated electoral reforms, such as the referendum, and State Socialism.

In 1870, the New Democracy disbanded, and its members joined the International as sections 9 and 12, of New York. Section 12, under the leadership of two sisters,

Victoria Woodhull and Tennessee Claflin,[36] well-known advocates of "social freedom," quickly became famous. It turned its attention to all sorts of extraneous matters, such as a "universal language," woman suffrage, "freedom of sexual relations." This imperiled the very successful propaganda of the Central Committee among labor organizations. Section 12 pursued its activities in the name of the International, refusing to recognize the authority of the Central Committee, and appealing to the General Council in London to become the leading Section in America — which was rejected. Finally, the foreign sections decided to put a stop to the activities of Section 12. The delegates of fourteen sections met and dissolved the Central Committee, reorganizing under the name of the Federal Council, and excluding Section 12 and a few sympathizing sections, which they offered admittance on the basis of the following propositions:

1. Only the labor question to be treated in the organization.

---

[36]Sisters, Victoria Woodhull (1838-1927) and Tennessee Claflin (1844-1923) were leading feminists and political activists, known as the first women to operate a brokerage firm on Wall Street. Victoria Woodhull became the first woman to run for president in 1872 when she ran as the candidate of the Equal Rights Party, on a ticket with abolitionist leader Frederick Douglass. The sisters established a newspaper, *Woodhull & Clafin's Weekly*, which was the first paper in America to print *The Communist Manifesto*. (A.K.B.)

2. Only new sections to be admitted two thirds of whose members are wage laborers.

3. Section 12 to be excluded, as strangers to the labor movement.

Section 12, being entirely composed on intellectuals, refused. The German sections called a national convention to legalize their coup d'état. The General Council in London made an investigation, and in 1872 Section 12 was expelled from the International. But Section 12 and its followers refused to accept the decision, and called a national convention of its own, in which were represented thirteen Sections, mostly English-speaking. This convention denounced the interference of the General Council in American affairs, and declared its intention to appeal to the General Congress of the International, at the Hague, in 1872.

Although Section 12 and its adhering Sections opposed the Marxians, they did not ally themselves with Bakunin and his action — although at the Hague Congress Bakunin supported the delegates of Section 12, who were expelled with him from the International. The new organization, dominated by Section 12, turned its attention to politics. At the same time, the convention of the regular International in America proclaimed as its intention "to rescue the working classes from the influence and power of all political parties, and show that the existence of all these parties is a crime and a threat against the working classes." It did not recognize that the time was yet ripe for political action.

In the Hague Congress, Sorge,[37] representing the orthodox Marxian organization in America, gave as his reason why the native American Sections were not entitled to representation, *that the native Americans were practically all speculators, while the immigrants alone constituted the wage-earning class in America.*

The headquarters of the International was transferred to New York in 1873. From then, strife developed within its ranks, until the convention of 1874, when the two opposing conceptions of political action pure and simple, as against the organization of trade unions as a basis for political action, again split the American International, and the political actionists permanently withdrew, and started the Social Democratic Party of North America. At the same time, the Labor Party of Chicago was formed.

In Europe, too, the workingmen were building up political parties in place of federations of the International. And this had its effect upon the American labor movement. But the chief reasons for the tendency toward political organization were the disastrous effects of the panic of 1873, which practically destroyed the American trade union

---

[37]Friedrich A. Sorge (1828-1906) was a German communist leader who emigrated to the United States in 1852. He played an important role in the American labor movement and helped to found the Socialist Labor Party of America. (A.K.B.)

movement, and *a desire to make Socialism more attractive to the American workers* — that is, to the small property holders.

But, at the same time, the American workingmen were perfecting the first of their powerful economic organizations, the two even then beginning their struggle for mastery on the industrial field — the Knights of Labor and the craft union movement. Politically, the rank and file of both these organizations were entirely impregnated with petit-bourgeois psychology. The Pittsburgh General Labor Convention of 1876 was captured by the Knights of Labor, who endorsed Greenbackism, from cheap money to the protective tariff, and thus cut adrift from the Socialists, who withdrew from the convention.

The result was to unite the Socialist factions, which came together and adopted a declaration of principles taken from the General Statutes of the International, and organized the Workingmen's Party of the United States,[38] which immediately plunged into politics.

My purpose in thus reviewing the early history of the American Socialist movement in detail, is to call attention to the nature of its action in the American political structure. Of course, it is obvious that the influence of Socialism upon the American state up to 1880 was necessarily small, because

---

[38]Founded in 1876, the Workingman's Party of the United States was influenced by Marxist political thought. It evolved into the Socialist Labor Party of America. (A.K.B.)

the movement itself was overshadowed by other political movements. Still, at a time when movements in Europe very similar in size and importance were having an important effect upon the policies of various governments, the effect in America was absolutely nil.

Why? I have tried to point out in this series of articles the disastrous effect of political democratic ideology upon the growth of class-consciousness. Even after the capitalist class in America had learned that government is not carried on in legislatures, but in banks and Chambers of Commerce, the workers still believed that political democracy could solve the problems of the wage-earners. This belief affected and modified the revolutionary theories imported from Europe. And when it did not, the class-conscious workingmen's organizations soon found that the capitalist political parties, with their appeal to small property holders, were easily able to capture the labor vote from the Socialists.

And finally, although, as Sorge stated at the Hague Congress, "the foreign immigrants alone constituted the wage-earning class in America," they found themselves unable in any way to bring influence upon the government or the ruling classes *because they were foreigners.*

This is as true today as it was in 1876 — if not more so, on account of the war. The foreign workers in this country are virtually excluded from all participation in the government, although they constitute the majority of the American working class. Although naturalized citizens, the latest immigration laws nullify this advantage, because under them citizenship can be revoked upon conviction of having revolutionary ideas. Their organizations are powerless; their press is muzzled; the courts convict them of political offenses upon the slightest evidence, and Organized Labor — as typified in the A.F. of L. — bars them from the advantages of even the inadequate labor organizations formed to defend the workers' economic interests.

The present outlawing of Socialists in politics, because they are Socialists, indicates the answer of the democratic State to the political action of the class-conscious workers.

V.

The formation of the Workingmen's Party marked the beginning of Socialism as a political force in the United States. The old distinctions of Internationalism and Lasalleanism gave way to the native American conflict between Trade Unionism and Politics — which continued to sway the movement from one side to another until the last generation.

So far, I have described the background of the movement in this country. With the Union Congress of 1876, Socialism entered upon the political arena in the struggle for power against the capitalist class.

A few sections locally entered political campaigns, and the resulting vote was so encouraging that others prepared to follow. Then came the nation-wide strikes of 1877, the activity of the sections in the strikes, the violence of the police, especially in Chicago, where a meeting of striking cabinetmakers was fired on. The National Executive Committee saw its opportunity, and ordered the sections to hold mass meetings endorsing labor demands. The autumn elections in many parts of the country showed a large Socialist vote. Immediately a special convention of the Party was called to define its attitude toward politics.

This convention met in December 1877 and remodeled its Declaration of Principles to the effect that "political action is the natural function of the Party." However, owing to the influence of the Trade Unionists, it declared also that the Party "should maintain friendly relations with the trade unions and should promote their formation upon socialistic principles." The name was changed to Socialistic Labor Party and a few years later, to Socialist Labor Party.

In the spring elections, a curious paradox was observable. In localities where the Trade Unionists were supreme, the candidates, who had been forced into politics by the Party policy, polled large votes because the unions supported them and worked for them; while in the districts where the pure Political Actionists predominated, the Labor vote went to the Greenbackers of the Republicans.

In the next national and state elections, the same phenomenon prevailed. The Chicago section, the most powerful in the country, elected four members to the legislature, who were influential enough to compel the appointment of an Industrial Commission, and the following year, secured four aldermen. In St. Louis, three Socialist candidates were elected to the legislature. But the drawbacks of the situation were made clear by the effects of the boom of 1879; prosperity drew the attention of labor away from politics, and the membership and vote of the Socialist Labor Party rapidly declined.

In 1880, the Political Actionists, in view of the diminishing Party vote, forced through a referendum to send delegates to the Greenback Convention in Chicago, and support the candidates of the Greenback Party. This compromise was passionately opposed by the Trade Unionists of Chicago, as well as by a group of revolutionary Socialists in New York, whose center was a handful of refugees from the German anti-Socialists laws.

Since the first campaign of the Workingmen's Party, the Trade Unionists had never abandoned their instinctive distrust of political action. In 1877-78, it is true, the election of candidates to municipal and state legislatures was of considerable agitational value. The state was not yet clearly defined as a direct instrument of capitalist exploitation; the Socialist legislators took it by surprise. But from then on, gangs of armed thugs invaded the polling places on election day; Socialist speakers were attacked; Socialist votes were torn up; and in Chicago, in 1879, the only Socialist alderman elected was deliberately refused his seat by the corrupt Democratic Council.

In 1879-80, as today, the lawless brutalities of the ruling class in nullifying the Socialist vote created a widespread disgust with political action. Already many workingmen's military organizations had sprung up to protect the Socialists from attack. The Political Actionists in control of the National Executive Committee repudiated these armed societies. The "deal" with the Greenback Party was the last straw for the Trade Union faction, which, with its growing system of labor organizations armed for defense, broke away from the Political Actionists, and, in 1881, issued a call to "all revolutionists and armed workingmen's organizations in the country," pointing out the necessity of "getting ready to offer an armed resistance to the invasions by the capitalist class and capitalist legislatures."

In October of the same year, a convention of revolutionists met at Chicago, and formed the Revolutionary Socialist Party, which rejected all political action and endorsed the so-called Black International, the anarchist International Working People's Association, declaring that it stood "ready to render armed resistance to encroachments upon the rights of workingmen." Before the referendum was completed, however, the Chicago section took part in one more municipal campaign, whose effect upon the Socialists was so disastrous that it destroyed the last vestige of faith in *even the agitational value of political campaigns.*

The Convention of 1883, at Pittsburgh, defined the two currents in the new organization; that led by Spies of Chicago, recognized revolutionary trade unionism – and that led by Johann Most of New York, advocating pure revolutionary anarchism. A compromise between the two was reached, resulting in a philosophy of organization and action almost analogous to modern Syndicalism.

It was under the influence of this organization that the great labor upheaval of 1885-86 took place, centering around the Eight-hour strikes, and culminating in the Haymarket Bombs of the Summer of 1886, which broke the Black International.[39]

The provocation of the ruling class which resulted in the explosions (analogous to the San Francisco bomb cases and the recent Post Office bombs), demonstrate to what lengths the capitalists will go in order to wreck all efforts of the workers to free themselves. *It is impossible to capture the capitalist state for the workers by means of the ballot*; this has been demonstrated again and again; and yet when Labor repudiates political action, it is met with fearful violence...

During this time the Socialist Labor Party had almost disappeared, not emerging until the Henry George[40] campaign of 1886 in New York, when the Socialists saw their opportunity to arouse the worker masses to political action once more, the result of which, they thought, would be to

---

[39]The Haymarket Massacre took place in Chicago on May 4, 1886. During labor protests in support of an eight-hour workday, a bomb was tossed when police tried to break up the demonstration, killing seven police officers and four civilians. (A.K.B.)

[40]Henry George (1839-1897) was an American political economist who proposed a single tax on land. He is considered the most famous American economic writer of the nineteenth century. His book, *Progress and Poverty* sold millions of copies around the world. (A.K.B.)

win the new movement to Socialism. But the Henry George movement concentrated on Single Tax, and finally repudiated Socialism; so, the Socialists threw their strength into the Progressive Labor Party, in New York. All over the country independent Labor Parties sprang up, and for a time the political results were astonishing. These Labor Parties elected no less than ten Congressmen, many legislators, judges, etc. Even in New York State, where the vote was small, the effect upon the legislature was such that a great quantity of labor legislation was enacted.

An attempt was made, in 1887, to combine these scattered parties into one national organization, which was accomplished by the Cincinnati Convention, wherein were included the Knights of Labor, the Farmers' Alliance, Greenbackers, etc. Here was launched the National Union Labor Party; but this turned out to be merely another "deal" with Greenbackism — the farmers (the small property holders) captured the organization, and the Socialists did not support it, nor did the industrial workers vote for it.

In 1888, began anew within the ranks of the Socialist Labor Party the old bitter fight between the Political Actionists and the Trade Unionists. In 1889, the Political Actionists on the National Executive Committee were replaced by Trade Unionists, and the Party placed itself behind the Eight-hour Movement, and promised support to the Unions. A minority of the sections revolted, organized their own machinery, and declared for pure political action.

This was known as the "Cincinnati Socialist Labor Party," in 1897 it amalgamated with the Debs-Berger Social Democracy of America, which was a combination of the political expression of the old American Railway Union, and the Populism of Berger. The new Party immediately plunged into politics.

In the meanwhile, the Socialist Labor Party was passing through a rapid evolution in its relations to organized labor. The gradual consolidation of the craft union, wage-conscious philosophy of the American Federation of Labor finally led to a battle in the old Central Labor Union of New York. The Socialist Labor Party set up an opposition body, the Central Labor Federation, which was refused a charter by the A.F. of L., and finally definitely expelled. Then, under the leadership of Daniel DeLeon,[41] the Socialist Labor Party attempted to capture the Knights of Labor. Using the United Hebrew Trades as his instrument, DeLeon got control of District Assembly 49, and then ousted Powderly as President of the Knights, and elected Sovereign. But Sovereign played him false. Beaten in both of the great labor organizations, DeLeon started his own Socialist Labor Party organization, to compete with the two — the Socialist Trade and Labor Alliance.

---

[41]Daniel DeLeon (1852-1914) was a socialist newspaper editor, trade union organizer, and a leading figure of the Socialist Labor Party of America. (A.K.B.)

Indirectly, this was the chief cause of the formation of the Socialist Party. A group in the Socialist Labor Party — called the "kangaroos" — were against the policy of combatting the labor organizations from without. They favored the policy of "boring" from within.

This meant to capture the A.F. of L. — at the time supreme — by working within the Unions to elect officials, and through them to dominate the membership.

In 1889, the "kangaroos" seceded from the Socialist Labor Party, and in 1900 they joined the Social Democracy — the new Party took the name of Socialist Party of America.[42] In the campaign of 1900, the Socialist Party rolled up a vote of almost 90,000, while the Socialist Labor Party's vote dwindled.

With the foundation of the Socialist Party, the history of the Socialist Labor Party, as a movement of the workers at grips with the capitalists on the political field, comes to an end. Henceforth the Socialist Labor Party is identified with the development of a great Socialist theoretician, Daniel

---

[42]Established in 1901, the Socialist Party of America following a merger between the Social Democratic Party of America and dissident elements from the Socialist Labor Party of America. It became the most successful socialist party in the history of the United States. Its presidential candidate, Eugene V. Debs, twice received over 900,000 votes in the 1912 and 1920 elections. It elected two members to the House of Representatives and numerous local officials. The party was dissolved in 1972. (A.K.B.)

DeLeon. The last attempt of the Socialist Labor Party to annex the labor movement occurred in 1905-07, in connection with the I.W.W., and resulted once more in the secession of the S.L.P. and the formation of a rival organization.

In the light of recent history, when the relatively enormous Socialist vote has failed to influence seriously the make-up of capitalist legislature, it will be a surprise to many persons to read of the legislative victories of the small and strife-torn Socialist movements of early days — small as they were in comparison with the huge spread and power of the capitalist system. But capitalism had not yet consolidated its hold on the State; the independent ballot was still a power — although even forty years ago could be discerned the answer of the ruling class to any challenge of its hegemony on the political or industrial field — violence.

The political power of the working class increased slowly; the bourgeois dictatorship of society grew by leaps and bounds; today the citadel of great capitalism is impregnable to all assaults except the mass assault of the united working class.

VI

The foundation of the Socialist Party of America proved that Socialism had become acclimatized. Born of Populism, Greenbackism, and Trade Unionism, it was grafted on to a Socialist tradition whose most important ancestor had been the teachings of Ferdinand Lasalle, imported into this country shortly after the Civil War. It was dominated by the prevailing American belief that the ballot controlled the State, and that the State could be conquered for the working class by the ballot. At the beginning, it was still revolutionary — that is to say, it aimed at the capture of political power. At hand it had a native economic organization of the workers — the American Federation of Labor — already grown powerful. Instead of trying to create a rival labor organization, it realized that this was impossible, and set out to capture for Socialism the organization already existing.

In all respects, therefore, the Socialist Party was apparently equipped to enter the political struggle with the capitalist class for power. And this it proceeded to do at once, with results which justified its belief that at last the combination had been discovered by which Socialism could be made attractive to American workmen.

The first national campaign — that of 1900 — tabulated 87,814 votes for the Socialist Party. Debs, who was very popular with the workers because of his activities in the American Railway Union, made a series of spectacular campaigns for the Presidency, culminating in 1912 with the country-wide tour of the "Red Special," when the Party rolled up almost a million votes. And this last campaign was carried on in the face of Roosevelt's dramatic crusade for "social justice," wherein the Progressive Party had incorporated many of the planks from the Socialist platform.

At the same time, the Socialists in various parts of the country elected several members of State Legislatures, city aldermen, and administrative officials. The most striking example of Socialist political success was in the city of Milwaukee, where Berger[43] was elected Alderman-at-Large, and finally Emil Seidel was elected Mayor, with a large proportion of the City Council composed of Socialists. For a time, indeed, Milwaukee was looked up to by American Socialists as a shining example of what Socialist political action could do — just as, before the war, Germany dominated the International because of its powerful party organization and its millions of votes.

---

[43]Victor L. Berger (1860-1929) became the first Socialist elected to the U.S. House of Representatives in 1910. He emigrated from Austria-Hungary in 1881 and settled in Milwaukee, Wisconsin. (A.K.B.)

The real emergence of Socialism upon the arena of the political fight, however, did not occur until 1910, when Victor Berger was elected Member of the House of Representatives for the Fifth Wisconsin District, and for the first time a representative of the Party of the working-class took his seat in the Congress of the United States, the highest law-making body. He sat for two terms; and then, after a lapse of two years, Meyer London of New York succeeded him as Representative, to be followed again in 1918 by the re-election of Berger.

It is not necessary here to go into the record of Victor Berger as first Congressional Representative of the working class Party.

His first act was to cast his vote for a substitute to the direct election of Senators. His maiden speech contained not one single reference either to the Socialist International or to the interest of the working-class as such; it was a purely reformist criticism of the capitalist state. The most salient feature of his tenure of office was the introduction of mild social reform legislation, of which his Old Age Pension bill is characteristic. For example, the pension was to accrue only after the worker's sixtieth year — and it is a well-known fact that the average life of an American industrial worker is forty years. It was to be denied to anyone convicted of a "felony" — even such a "felony" as that of which Victor Berger now stands convicted by the capitalist courts. It was to be denied to anyone, no matter how old, who had an income of six dollars per week. And finally, all "unnaturalized aliens", which compose the vast majority of the most exploited section of the American working class, were barred.

Add to this, Berger's opposition to Woman Suffrage, on the ground that women were largely dominated by religion, and would therefore strengthen the reactionary political forces; and later, his advocacy of intervention in Mexico; and we have a picture of a man in some respects less revolutionary than the bourgeois Jeffersonian Liberals.

In full consciousness of the desperate situation in which Victor Berger now finds himself, and in full respect to his courage, I do not wish to misquote Berger or misstate his position. I shall therefore quote extracts from his recent pamphlet, "Open Letter Addressed to His Colleagues in Congress", in order that he may speak for himself:

> I am one of the founders of the Socialist Party of America.... I have always prided myself on strict obedience to laws, even when I do not like them....

> The American Socialists were opposed to our entry into the war, but so were many Republicans and Democrats in and out of Congress...

> The American Socialists held to the wise counsel of George Washington, Thomas Jefferson, James Monroe and Abraham Lincoln- to keep out of European troubles...

That is the reason why we demanded legislation depriving any citizen or corporation of all profits from the sale of war supplies for the American government.

Many Republicans and Democrats believed and said the same...

Now Socialism is not Bolshevism.

Socialism is the collective ownership of the means of social production and distribution — while Bolshevism, as far as I understand it, is Communism combined with syndicalism.

The Communists want to produce and consume in common...

Socialism, however, wants to control only productive capital — not all property. A Socialist commonwealth will not do away with the individual ownership of property, but only with the individual ownership of socially necessary capital.

Communism denies individual ownership of all property.

The Bolshevists discourage parliamentary action.

They prefer direct action and the dictatorship of the proletariat.

The Bolshevists want to break entirely with the past and start anew. The Socialists do not believe that a complete break is either possible or desirable.

If we are to remain a politically free people the inevitable outcome must be that the people must take possession collectively of the social means of production and distribution — and use them for the nation as a whole — and that is called Socialism.

The measures that the Socialists will take — must closely connect with the present system and evolve from it.

The Socialists believe that everything that is necessary for the life of the nation — for the enjoyment of everybody within the nation — the nation is to own and manage.

Everything that is necessary for the life and development of the state — the state is to own and manage.

Everything that is necessary for the life and development of the city — the city is to own and manage....

Everything that the individual can own and manage best — the individual is to own and manage. There will be plenty of enterprises left for the initiative of the individual.

This is nothing but State Capitalism in its most complete form. Mr. Hearst will cheerfully endorse it. In it, there is not a word to indicate that the proletariat must control the State, and that it must, as Marx points out, break down the capitalist State apparatus and rebuild anew the entire machinery of government and of production. There is very little difference between this ideal and the industrial organization of Imperial Germany before the war.

Meyer London's career in Congress began little better. In a speech supporting the Jones bill giving citizenship to the Puerto Ricans, London threatened that if Congress denied the ballot to these people, it would be placing in their hands "the bomb of the revolutionist and the assassin's knife." Immediately, the House was in an uproar; the members sternly threatened that they would discipline the Socialist Congressman unless he withdrew his remarks, so Socialist Congressman Meyer London *apologized and ate his words.*

From that time on, outside of a few speeches concerning the housing situation in the District of Columbia and other minor matters of that sort, Congressman London remained silent. On the resolution declaring war on Germany, he voted "nay." On the military appropriation, however, he *did not vote.* Finally, the fearful pressure engendered by the war, and the savage patriotic persecution in the Congress beat down his half-hearted resistance; so that, in 1918, he was the Congressman selected to deliver an address of eulogy commemorating the third anniversary of Italy's entrance into the war.

Taken to task by his comrades in New York for his chauvinistic utterances, Comrade London declared that although born a foreigner, he had been made in America, and he would be true to his country; furthermore, he added that he was responsible to all his constituents — and that these constituents were not only Socialists (working men) but *all the people of his district.* The disastrous records of Socialists elected to office are endless.

Mayor Seidel of Milwaukee appointed many non-Socialists to posts in the city administration, and when criticized, declared that he represented all the people — not merely the Socialist Party. Mayor Lunn of Schenectady did the same thing; when taken to task for his un-Socialistic behavior, the Mayor proudly resigned from the Socialist Party — but remained Mayor, and afterward became one of the chief pro-War Democratic Congressmen. Mayor Van Lear of Minneapolis, after election to office of an anti-War program, joined Samuel Gompers' Alliance for Labor and Democracy, which was formed by the reactionaries of the American Federation of Labor to support the War; and when the Non-Partisan League put up a candidate in a local election, Mayor Van Lear made a public speech in favor of this candidate, although a candidate of his own Party was running. His last act in office was to refuse to veto a Red Flag law passed by the City Council of Minneapolis *against the Socialists.*

But, after all, it is not these examples of the failure of Socialist officials in office which forms the most damning demonstration of the failure of old-style Socialist political action. The War intensified and brought out the real nature of political power and control. For example, in cases where the Socialists in office actually tried to follow Socialist principles, capitalist action was swift and merciless. In Minneapolis, for instance, Mayor Van Lear having manifested a mild hospitality toward free speech, the State government promptly took away his police power and governed the city through the State Council of National Defense, which was composed of the representatives of big business. Mayor Hoan, Socialist Mayor of Milwaukee, was completely divested of his power as a city executive by the business interests of Wisconsin acting through the Governor and Council of National Defense. In Cleveland, two Socialists were elected to the City Council; one was disbarred, because a woman reported that twelve months before he had been heard to say that he did not believe in the Red Cross — and the other Councilman was expelled *because he belonged to the same political Party as his colleague.* Victor Berger ran for United States Senate in Wisconsin in the Spring of 1918. In order to prevent him from taking his seat, the business interests of his State and of the country at large secured his indictment in the Federal Courts, on charges much less grave than those upon which many Socialists had already been acquitted. Berger then ran for the House of Representatives. This was the signal for still further indictments. He was elected by an overwhelming vote — and another indictment was clapped upon him; and after the armistice had been signed, Berger was tried and convicted, and sentenced to twenty years in jail.

At the height of the Socialist Party's career, in 1912, more than nine hundred thousand votes were cast for its presidential candidate — *about one-fifteenth of the entire vote cast for President, and one-sixth of the ballots cast for Woodrow Wilson, the winning candidate.* Roughly, the Democratic and Republican electorate was represented in Congress proportionally to their presidential vote; but the Progressives — the Party of the rebel small property owners — was not represented in proportion to its vote; *and the*

Socialists, with one-fifteenth of all the ballots, got one Congressman, although on the face of it they were entitled to about thirty. True, many Congressional Districts had no elections in 1912; but this does not alter the essential truth of this statement. In Europe, the development of such political strength by any party would have immediately showed in the legislative body; this is true even in Germany, in spite of restrictions to the franchise. But in America it can be readily seen that, although political democracy more or less accurately reflects the comparative strength of the bourgeois parties, it operates to block the adequate representation of all classes contending with the great capitalists for State control.

Why is this so? Why is it that in Europe the political Socialist movement was able to develop great strength in the legislative bodies, and exercise an important influence on the Governments?

This results from the fact that *nowhere in the world is the capitalist class so strongly organized and so firmly intrenched as in America.* In America, from the first, the capitalist class controlled the State, and there was no other class in society except the working class. In Europe, the capitalist class had to fight against the remnants of the feudal class. Almost up to the Great War, in some parts of Europe there was a dual revolution going on: the capitalists were striving with the dying feudal system to gain control of the State, and the rising proletariat was also beginning to battle for power.

Both feudal class and capitalists used the working class against each other, and thus the Socialists became an important factor between the two contending class-factions. And thus, above all, the capitalists were compelled to fight in two directions at once, and in the meanwhile, to give concessions to the working class in return for its aid against the feudal system.

In America, however, there was no feudal class to divert the capitalists from their war against the working class. More than that, the ballot enabled the American capitalist class to blind the workers with illusions of "democracy" until they had perfected their hold upon the throat of the republic.

For the last decade the history, the American Socialist Party has shown a continuous tendency to draw away from the proletariat. The policy of "boring from within" in the American Federation of Labor resulted in the virtual capture of the Party, for a period, by the Federation — which by that time had become a definitely wage-conscious, anti-Socialist, counter-revolutionary, reformistic body. The split with the I.W.W. in 1912, by the adoption of Article Two, Section Six, in the Party constitution, finally completely separated the Party from the revolutionary American proletariat, and forced out of the Party some of its best elements.

The Party platforms became so filled with reformist demands calculated to appeal to professionals and small property owners, that the Progressive Party adopted several of them in 1912. For the moment, this did not effectually modify the Socialist vote; but when, four years later, under the threat of war, the Wilson Democrats adopted the same tactics, it proved fatal to the Party — the Presidential vote fell almost one-half.

The St. Louis War Resolution,[44] forced upon the Party officialdom by the rank and file, gave promise of a new spirit in the Socialist movement, born of the shock of war. But how the Party officials and office-holders violated or apologized for the St. Louis Resolution, and what happened to the members of the rank and file who attempted to live up to it, reminds one of the leaders of the Second International, and the millions of trusting workers betrayed by them.

The War revealed the power of capitalist political control. Before it, the political workingmen's parties disappeared, were overwhelmed by the parliaments in which they participated, by the machinery of political democracy which they helped to maintain....

---

[44]See note 1. (A.K.B.)

VII

Having in former articles traced the failure of the small property holders, Labor and the Socialists to gain control of the Government in America, it is now necessary to indicate how the few great capitalists are able, in the most advanced political democracy of the world, to withstand the pressure of all other classes, either alone or combined — in other words, just how political democracy fails to assure a government by the majority.

When Karl Marx said that the modern capitalist state was "*nothing less than a machine for the oppression of one class by another, and that not less so in a democratic republic than under a monarchy,*" he made a profound observation, the more remarkable since at that time the origin of political democratic states was still surrounded with a romantic halo of libertarian phrases — which still inspired the Forty-Eighters.

Fortunately, thanks to the work of Beard, McMaster, and others, the origins of the American Republic are today available to all;[45] and they demonstrate with utter clearness that *the Government of the United States was designed by its founders to protect the rich against the poor, property against the necessities of life and liberty, and the monopolistic minority against the majority.*

Pre-Revolutionary society in America was divided into three very sharply-defined classes: the upper class consisting of the clergy, professional men, merchants, landed proprietors and the great slave-holding planters in the South; the middle class, of shop keepers and farmers; and the comparatively unimportant lower class, of slaves, poor whites in the South, mechanics, indentured servants and apprentices — all of which had no votes. Except among the middle and lower classes, there was no discontent with the political institutions of the British Empire; on the other hand, there was a healthy contempt for Democracy, often expressed, among the well-to-do and educated.

Until the acts of the British Government began seriously to hamper *trade* — in other words, *property* — the upper class in the American colonies was not in any sense revolutionary; in fact, many of the framers of the Constitution had been *against* the Revolution. In any sense, the Revolution, for the Colonial upper class, was favored only insofar as it

---

[45]John B. McMaster, *History of the People of the United States from the Revolution to the Civil War* (8 Vols.) (1883); Charles Beard, *An Economic Interpretation of the Constitution of the United States* (1913). (A.K.B.)

promised to protect their material interests. Like all Revolutions, however, it was precipitated and expressed by idealists, and carried through by the masses — in this case, the middle class — who saw in it the opportunity to establish a government in their own interests. These interests were expressed in the formula, "Life, Liberty and the Pursuit of Happiness" — which did not refer to slaves and indentured servants at all, but to the vast majority of traders and farmers.

This was the element which wrote the Declaration of Independence, in the heat of the Revolutionary struggle, when, as in all Revolutions, the mass was dictating the slogans of the movement.

The eleven years of the confederation which followed, however, proved that human society was definitely embarked on the capitalist era, which was incompatible with those "natural rights" — that individualistic liberty so fondly embraced by the small property owners, as best suiting their free development in a land of unequalled opportunity.

The middle class whose services in the Revolutionary struggle had made them the dominant class in society, were jealous of their freedom and independence. Already the development of capitalism had begun to concentrate wealth in the hands of a few. Great corporations had already tied up immense tracts of land, and the banking interests in the towns had a monopoly of capital; these conditions had made the petty bourgeoisie a debtor class. The middle class therefore was in favor, as at later periods, of cheap currency, and of the violability of contracts. A small group of capitalists had secured control of the depreciated Congressional and State obligations issued to pay for the Revolution, and the middle class wished to wipe out this debt. And just as the great capitalists were in favor of a strongly centralized government, which would guarantee their speculative investments and mortgages, and protect this property with federal troops and police, so the middle class feared a centralized government, whose actions it might not be able to control as it controlled the separate state legislatures.

Attempts at oligarchy or dictatorship in each separate state might be opposed, if all other means failed, by a popular uprising. In fact, the eleven years of the Confederation saw many such insurrections. It is interesting to note here that *these Insurrections were directed against the capitalists, who had got control of the state governments, by the middle class debtors.* The culminating insurrection was Shays' Rebellion.[46]

---

[46]Shays' Rebellion, led by Revolutionary War veteran Daniel Shays was a rebellion against excessive state taxation. As the federal government was unable to raise funds to suppress the rebellion, which was ultimately quelled by state and private militia, it served as a catalyst to replace the Articles of Confederation in a Constitutional Convention. (A.K.B.)

The situation is well described by Mr. Curtis, in his *Constitutional History of the United States:*[47]

> "A levelling, licentious spirit," says this old reactionary, "a restless desire for change, and a disposition to throw down barriers of private rights, at length broke forth in conventions, which first voted themselves to be the people and then declared their proceedings to be constitutional. At these assemblies the doctrine was publicly broached *that property ought to be common*, because all had aided in saving it from confiscation by the power of England. Taxes were voted to be unnecessary burdens, the courts of justice to be intolerable grievances, and the legal profession a nuisance. A revision of the State constitution was demanded, in order to abolish the Senate, reform the representation of the people, and make all civil officers eligible by the people..."

It was these revolts which furnished the immediate incentive to the adoption of the Constitution. The work of preparing the country for the capitalist *coup d'état* had been carried on carefully and tactfully for several years by Alexander Hamilton and James Madison — afterward President of the United States. In calling the Constitutional Convention of 1787, for instance, the leaders did not dare to suggest their real objects; the aim of the Convention, it was stated, was merely "to revise the Articles of Confederation." It was also carefully arranged that the delegates should not

---

[47]George T. Curtis, *History of the Origin, Formation, and Adoption of the Constitution of the United States* (2 vols.) (1854, 1861). (A.K.B.)

be elected by the people, or even by directly representative bodies, as had been done in the case of the Congress which issued the Declaration of Independence; instead, they were either chosen by the legislatures, or, more often, appointed by the Governors of the states. And it should be remembered that property qualification for the franchise existed in all the states, so that in no case was the lower, or working class, represented in the Convention.

And when the Convention finally met, it did its work in secret, behind closed doors, like the Peace Conference in Paris; and like the latter, in order to prevent the public from knowing what was going on, it even forced its members to promise not to talk to anyone outside. So that when the Constitution was finally completed, it was issued to the world in such a form that its real meaning, and the forces which produced it, were absolutely unknown to the colonists. The majority of the signers of the Declaration of Independence were Revolutionary leaders, men representing the small property holders; while the majority of the framers of the Constitution were the bankers, speculators in the land and money, and the merchants. Many delegates to the Constitutional Convention who had signed the Declaration of Independence refused to sign the Constitution, denouncing it as a "conspiracy"; among these was Benjamin Franklin.

James Madison, afterward President of the United States, who was chiefly responsible for the Constitution —

which he described as having "the form and spirit of popular government while preventing majority rule" — expressed, in 1785, the theory of economic interpretation in politics. He wrote:

> The most common and durable source of factions (parties, classes) has been the various and unequal distribution of property. Those who hold and those who are without property have ever formed distinct interests in society. Those who are creditors, and those who are debtors, fall under a like discrimination. A landed interest, a manufacturing interest, a mercantile interest, a moneyed interest, grow up of necessity in civilized nations and divide them into different classes, actuated by different sentiments and views. The regulation of these various and interfering interests forms the principal task of modern legislation, and involves the spirit of party and faction in the necessary and ordinary operations of the government.

It will be seen by this that before the end of the eighteenth century the American capitalist class had discovered, and applied for its own advantage, what Karl Marx discovered more than sixty years later.

Listen once more to Madison, speaking before the Constitutional Convention, advocating that the vote be given to the propertied classes alone:

> In future times a great majority of the people will not only be without land, *but any other sort of property*. These will either combine under the influence of their common situation; in which case, the rights of property and the public liberty will not be secured in their hands, or,

which is more probable, they will become the tools of opulence and ambition...

Elbridge Gerry declared that all the evils experienced by the Confederation flowed "from the excess of democracy." Edmund Randolph said, "that the general object was to provide a cure for the evils under which the United States labored; that, in tracing these evils to their origin, every man had found it in the turbulence and follies of democracy; that some check therefore was to be sought for against this tendency of our government..." Alexander Hamilton, in urging a life-term for Senators, said that *"all communities divide themselves into the few and the many. The first are the* rich and well-born, and the other the mass of the people who seldom judge or act right." Gouverneur Morris, of New York, wanted to check the precipitancy, changeableness, and excess" of the representatives of the people, by the ability and virtue of "great and established property-aristocracy; men who from pride will support consistency and permanency... Such an aristocratic body will keep down the turbulence of democracy." Governor Morris showed the capitalist viewpoint of the Convention, when he boldly stated, "Life and liberty were generally stated to be of more value than property. An accurate view of the matter would, nevertheless, prove that *property was the main object of society....* If *property, then, was the main object of government,* certainly it ought to be one measure of the influence due to those who were to be affected by the government." And finally, Mr. Madison again:

An increase of population will of necessity increase the proportion of those who will labor under all the hardships of life and secretly sigh for a more equal distribution of its blessings. These may in time outnumber those who are placed above the feelings of indigence. (The poor may outnumber the rich.) According to the equal laws of suffrage, the power will slide into the hands of the former. No agrarian attempts have yet been made in this country, but symptoms of a levelling spirit, as we have understood, have sufficiently appeared, in a certain quarter (Shays' Rebellion), to give notice of a future danger.

Madison further advised the Convention that in framing a system which they wished to last for ages, *they must not lose sight of the changes which the ages would produce in the forms and distribution of property.*

The Convention did not. It finally framed a Constitution, which, while appearing to preserve popular government, in reality secured the rights and property of the minority against "the superior force of an interested and overbearing majority."

Liberals and "parliamentary" Socialists in this country are always pleading for the "minority rights" guaranteed by the Constitution. But the "minority" which the Constitution guarantees is not the one they are talking about; it is the permanent capitalist minority, and it is guaranteed against the will of the majority.

This is accomplished through the so-called "check and balance system," by which the President is indirectly elected, the members of the House of Representatives are elected in one way, the Senate in another, and finally, the most powerful body of all, the Supreme Court, is not elected at all, but appointed.

These various bodies check each other's action so that no popular majority can control the processes of legislation, except after a long and tedious process. Today even this possibility is removed by the fact that the colossal financial interests absolutely own and control the government.

It is fascinating to study the history of these times — to discover, for instance, that most of the signers of the Constitution derived immediate personal wealth from its proclamation; that there was a conspiracy among the upper class of the colonies, in case the Convention failed, to organize an insurrection to overthrow "democracy" by force of arms; that out of the sixty-odd delegates elected, only thirty-nine signed the document, many withdrew from the Convention altogether, and an immense anger shook the middle class when it discovered, too late, what the Constitution meant; that the middle class had to threaten to refuse ratification before the first ten amendments, which constitute the Bill of Rights, were added to the document; and that the different state legislatures were persuaded to ratify the Constitution through the most shameless corruption by the capitalist interests — even going to the extent of bribery.

The first act of the new Government established by the Constitution, as was to be expected, was the "funding" of the public debt — that is to say, an arrangement to pay the badly depreciated state and Congressional obligations at their face value. This debt amounted to more than $76,000,000. The holders of the depreciated bonds and notes — most of which they had purchased for a song — were given in exchange bonds of the new Government of the United States, which then proceeded to levy taxes upon the middle and working classes to pay the interest and principal. Thus, at the very beginning of our Government, the little clique of bankers and speculators who framed the Constitution were given a vast fortune, the payment of which reduced the American people to the position of debtors for half a century.

Another way by which the Constitution-framers profited. Although pledged to secrecy in the Convention, they used their knowledge of the proceedings to speculate in land and government securities and currency, before knowledge was made public.

An analogy with the present situation regarding the Peace Treaty with Germany, which has got into the hands of the great financial interests before it has reached the people, will readily suggest itself...

The Constitution so devised has been the framework of the American Government, and has consistently thwarted the will of the majority of the people ever since it was adopted, except in cases of an overwhelming majority. Patrick Henry, upon reading the document, exclaimed, "It is, sir, a most fearful situation when the most contemptible minority can prevent the alteration of the most oppressive government; for it may, in many respects, prove to be such."

Professor Burgess[48] protests against the system for amending the Constitution, and in doing so, unwittingly criticizes the entire document:

> When in a democratic political society, the well-matured, long, and deliberately-formed will of the undoubted majority can be persistently and successfully thwarted, in the amendment of the organic law, by the will of the minority, there is just as much danger to the States from revolution and violence as there is from the caprice of the majority.

So much for the foundations of the American republic; so much for "the most advanced political democracy in the world." However, there have been times when the great capitalists in control of the Government deliberately violated the Constitution, when it suited their interests; for example, just after the Civil War, when the Republicans in Congress forbade the Supreme Court to pass upon some of their reconstruction legislation, *on pain of being dissolved.* Toward the working-class, however, the Supreme Court has

---

[48]John W. Burgess (1844-1931), renowned professor of political science at Columbia University, author of several books on constitutional law. (A.K.B.)

become more and more the obstructive instrument of capitalist class-interest, and the Constitution an ever greater weapon against the workers; even to the point where it has upheld the conviction of Eugene V. Debs.

From time to time, the Constitution has been amended, and its provisions interpreted, so as to widen and strengthen the political powers of the people in Government — in other words, our Government has become more "democratic."

But this is only in proportion as the great capitalists strengthen the Invisible Government, and as the processes of "political democracy" became less and less able to overthrow their absolute hegemony — in other words, the center of Government has finally shifted completely from the Capitol and the White House to Wall Street. This became clear during the Great War.

My next and last article of this series will point out some ways by which the American capitalist class preserves and strengthens its power.

VIII

In a previous article, I attempted to show the economic interests behind the Constitution of the United States, and the deliberate expedients employed by the Colonial ruling class to create a government which would obstruct the will of the majority of the people. Let us now briefly see how the machinery operates.

Contrary to general belief, the American political democracy is not one of the most advanced democratic governments of the world, but one of the most backward. To indicate a few points in which it lags behind other governments: The President is elected for four years, and cannot be removed except for serious cause, by impeachment; but the Premiers of England, France, and Italy, retire when their Party loses power. The Cabinet of the United States Government is not responsible to anyone, and can only be removed by the President, who appoints it; the Cabinets of England, France, and Italy are responsible to the parliaments, and fall with the Premier. Laws passed by Congress may be declared invalid by the Supreme Court; but laws passed by the British Parliament cannot be reviewed by any court, and can only be changed at the ballot-box. In the United States, the form of Government is rigidly fixed by the Constitution, which moreover eternally guarantees the sacredness of property — nor can this Constitution be altered except by an overwhelming majority, which practically makes impossible any profound economic change by law; while in England no such bar exists to Revolution by law.

However, these apparent differences in degree of political democracy are not so important as they seem. In all political democratic countries today, under the capitalist system, "*the State power is more and more turned into an organ of Capital's mastery over Labor — a public force organized for social enslavement, an engine of class despotism.*" In the United States, however, the methods by which the great capitalists control the State are more apparent to the observer than elsewhere; although here, too, the masses of the people are more blinded by the "democratic" ideology in which political concepts are phrased, and by what a great Frenchman called "the illusion of the ballot-box."

It must be admitted that the Constitution has been broadened during the last century — that more and more "democracy" has been introduced into our Government; such amendments as the Income Tax and the Direct Election of Senators testify to this tendency. Also, the evolution of the State constitutions, removing franchise restrictions; and the acts of Congress and the State legislatures, fixing the control and hastening the democratization of the electoral machinery — all these signify that larger and larger masses of citizens theoretically participate in the Government. *But these "democratic" advances exactly correspond with the growth of the Invisible Government* — the autocracy of finance — which progressively nullifies the power of the political ballot.

Political democratic ideals grew out of the theory that men were born free and equal; that their interests were ostensibly equal interests, resulting from freedom of opportunity — and that it was the conflict of these equal but diversified property rights — especially their *geographical* diversity — which made it possible to construct a government representing all and satisfying the great majority. Such conditions existed to a greater degree in the American Colonies, with their hinterland of undeveloped continent, and their lack of any indigenous aristocracy, than in other parts of the world, and the Declaration of Independence was the expression of these sentiments.

But even at the time of the War of Independence, the capitalist system was well-developed, and the Constitution, eleven years later, embodied the clear class-consciousness of the Colonial capitalists, rendered palatable by "democratic" idealistic phraseology.

Madison had warned the Convention to take into account the new and changing forms in which property would manifest itself in the future. In the next century, the industrial era brought into existence wholly new forms of property; and, moreover, changed both the relations of men to one another, and the relations of men to their Government. The ownership of the tools of production and the means of distribution by a few, reduced the mass of mankind to dependence upon these few for all the necessities of life.

Now the State is the expression of the relations of classes — property-relations — in society. The American Government, particularly, was formed to protect property; and since as time went on more and more wealth was concentrated in the hands of the few great capitalists, the Government protected and fostered this capitalist property more and more. The mass of mankind became dependent upon the will of the industrial autocrats for their very existence. When they combined and demanded a larger share of the product of their labor, this constituted an attack upon private property, and the Government was called in to suppress them. Important illustrations of this are the calling in of Federal troops during the Pullman strike in 1894;[49] the

---

[49]Led by Eugene V. Debs, president of the American Railway Union, Pullman Strike took place when employees of the Pullman Company went on strike to protest a reduction in wages. The strike shut down freight and passenger traffic in the western part of the U.S. The federal government stepped in and obtained an injunction against the Union. When the strikers refused to obey, President Grover Cleveland ordered in Federal troops to stop them from obstructing the trains. More than 30 people died in the violence, the Union was dissolved and Debs was imprisoned. (A.K.B.)

use of injunctions in industrial disputes, in some cases forbidding strikes — and in one important instance, *even forbidding the workers to stop working for a corporation*; the manipulation of laws directed against the great corporations — such as the Sherman Anti-Trust Law — so as to turn it against the working class — as in the case of labor boycotts (see the case of the Danbury Hatters[50]); and finally, the interpretation of laws by the Courts.

After all this innovation, unique among political democracies, has turned out to be the easiest and most successful expedient for thwarting the will of the masses, and defending the political power of the capitalist class. Founded with the ostensible purpose of interpreting the Constitution, the Supreme Court has extended its powers of "interpretation" until it has become, in fact, a legislative body in itself; and being composed largely of eminent corporation lawyers, it represents the most reactionary property interests. For instance, it declared unconstitutional a law passed by the New York State Legislature forbidding bakery employees to work more than ten hours a day — on

---

[50]The Danbury Hatters case refers to an attempt by the United Hatters of North America to organize a union in 1902 among workers at a hat factory in Danbury, Connecticut. When they failed, the Union organized a nationwide boycott of the company's products. The company then brought a suit under the Sherman Anti-Trust Act and, in 1908, was awarded damages. (A.K.B.)

the ground that this statute infringed the rights and liberties of manufacturers as citizens under the Constitution. It declared the Income Tax Law unconstitutional, and more recently the Child Labor Law — both because they were attacks upon "property" and "liberty." On the other hand, in spite of the Constitutional provision specifically forbidding Congress to make any law "abridging the freedom of speech," the Supreme Court upheld the conviction of Eugene V. Debs and Kate Richards O'Hare for expressing their opinions upon political questions.

The Federal judiciary has been the supreme authority in the Government, even dominating Congress — except when Congress fell into the hands of a new dominant class. For instance, in 1866, Congress passed the famous "reconstruction" acts, some of which were clearly unconstitutional. Congress had then been captured by the Northern Republicans, the new powerful great capitalists, under the leadership of Thaddeus Stevens, the iron manufacturer of Pennsylvania. In passing these acts, Congress warned the Supreme Court not to lay its hands on them; and the Supreme Court obeyed.

In other cases, the capitalists have used the President against Congress. In 1864, Lincoln, and the most far-seeing of the great industrial capitalists of the North, determined to abolish slavery — both as a military measure against the South and as a way of destroying the economic competition of slave-labor. The Thirteenth Amendment to the

Constitution was about to be submitted to the States for ratification, against a very determined opposition. It was seen that one more state was necessary for the ratification, and three votes were needed in Congress to admit Nevada into the Union. Lincoln did not hesitate to bribe three Congressmen by appointing them to Federal offices.

In 1906, the revolt of the small property owners against the headlong career of great capitalist trustification and monopolization had reached a stage when the small property owners had got control of Congress and placed on the statute books the Sherman Anti-Trust Law. The Supreme Court, after its experience with popular wrath awakened by the rejection of the Income Tax Law in 1905, did not dare to declare the Sherman Law unconstitutional. Here was a clear case of political democracy at work — the will of the majority. Blocked in its plan of absorbing the Tennessee Coal and Iron Company by this law, the great financiers who were forming the United States Steel Corporation deliberately precipitated the Panic of 1907. President Roosevelt was forced to beg for mercy from the great capitalists, who consented to stop the panic on condition of being permitted to proceed with their plans. In 1907-08, then, the Tennessee Coal and Iron Company was "absorbed," in direct violation of the law. In 1909, the Senate demanded that the Attorney-General inform it whether he had instituted proceedings against the Steel Trust, and if not, why not. President Roosevelt directed the Attorney-General *not to answer the Senate*; and further declared that the Cabinet was responsible to himself alone.

In spite of the will of the vast majority of voters in the country, expressed in the election of Wilson, and the passage of the Sherman and the Clayton Acts, the aggregation of vast groups of capital has gone on a pace, untouched by the law; or when the great combinations have been forced to dissolve — such as the Standard Oil — they have done so in appearance only, and the result has been, as everyone knows, merely to strengthen their monopolistic hold upon the resources of the country.

The war completed the abject surrender of the Government to the great financiers. The country — the voting majority of small property owners — elected the Democratic administration in 1916, primarily because "it had kept us out of war." But by the spring of 1917, the United States Government was at war. It had been clearly proven for almost two years that the forces which were pushing the country toward war were the great munitions interests, the bankers who had floated Allied loans, and the imperialist corporations anxious to share in the redistribution of foreign markets. The United States was by this time, through the action of private bankers, heavily involved in the Allied cause; the Allied blockade had cut off German commerce, and a vast trade had opened up with England, France, and Russia. Allied defeat would have proven disastrous to Wall Street, which, at the very moment that the Allied strength wavered, plunged America into the struggle.

Never had there appeared so clearly the almost complete control of the press and all agencies of publicity by the capitalist class; with one voice they bayed for bloodshed, repeating unanimously every rumor of German "atrocities." German propagandists here were outlawed; British and French propagandists bought, corrupted, threatened, pleaded without hindrance. Congressmen who dared to oppose war in the interest of their constituents were lashed with a bitter fury by press and pulpit and the President. I was at that time in Washington, lobbying against the war and against conscription. Three-fourths of the Congressmen admitted to me that they did not want war, that their constituents were against it; but almost all of them were terrified of the Chambers of Commerce (the business men, bankers, etc.) of their districts, and dared not brook the wrath of the great newspapers.

And when once the country had gathered way toward the great decision, and conscription had been passed, the great capitalists delivered their ultimatum to the cowering Government in Washington. The Anti-Trust legislation must be suspended; the bankers and business men themselves must run the war. Hence, we had the amazing spectacle of the Council of National Defense, made up of speculators, manufacturers and merchants, awarding Government Contracts at outrageous prices in the morning and in the evening accepting these same contracts as private individuals. But not only this: all through the country, Chambers of Commerce and Boards of Trade formed organizations of armed detectives and police, composed of business men and bankers, who used the power delegated to them by the Department of Justice to wage the class war against the Labor Movement. And an arbitrary War Labor Board legislated in all differences between capital and labor, whose decisions were binding and backed by the power of the Federal Government. The workers were forced to obey these decisions or forced into the army; the great corporations, most of them, either refused to obey decisions they did not like, or like the manufacturers of Bridgeport, Connecticut, took advantage of the war-situation to destroy the defenses of organized labor.

Advocates of parliamentary action often point to the mass of labor-legislation passed by Congress and the state legislatures, — such as eight-hour laws, workmen's compensation statutes, minimum wage regulations and factory laws in general. Like the increase in political "democracy," the increase in industrial "democracy" is also in exact ratio to the growth of knowledge among the great labor-employers that the more labor is protected, the more efficient it is; and the more it can produce, and the more it can be exploited. The speeding-up of machinery consequent upon mechanical perfection and scientific management now make it possible to exploit labor more thoroughly in eight hours, than in twelve hours. Lord Leverhulme, the English employer, now advocates the Six-Hour Day, because it is productive of larger profits for the manufacturer than the Eight-Hour Day....

But when the capitalist does not feel it to his interest to obey the law, he does not obey it; and the State backs him up in his disobedience. For example, in Colorado there has been an eight-hour law on the Statute-books for twenty years or more; and yet, in 1913, that law was deliberately broken in the coal-mines of the state, and had been for ten years. All attempts of the men themselves to organize for its enforcement were frustrated by armed force. The unions were smashed by armed thugs, who killed and deported miners at will. At election time the ballot boxes were placed on company ground, guarded by armed hirelings of the coal companies, and no one allowed to vote who did not vote right. If anyone voted the wrong ticket, or was found by the company spies to be talking organization or any other heresy, he lost his job, was ousted from his house (company property) and run out of the town (which was also built on company property). And when at last the miners struck, the State Government sent the militia to break the strike, and this militia, the official police of the State, set fire to the strikers' tent-colony and burned women and children to death. The strikers' leaders were tried for murder; the gunmen and militiamen went free.

In San Francisco, the Chamber of Commerce determined to crush Organized Labor on the Pacific Coast. Someone planted a bomb which exploded in the Preparedness Parade, killing and wounding many people. Tom Mooney, his wife, Israel Weinberg, and a few other men active in the labor movement were arrested, and on perjured evidence Tom Mooney[51] was sentenced to death. Before he could be hanged, it was discovered that the whole business was a frame-up, that the evidence had been manufactured by the District Attorney in collusion with the Chamber of Commerce. The President's Investigating Commission recommended freedom or a new trial for Mooney. But the Governor of California, at the instigation of the Chamber of Commerce, simply commuted Mooney's sentence to life imprisonment. And there he lies a life prisoner though Innocent; while such is the power of the California capitalists, that Hiram Johnson, Senator from California, does not dare raise his voice to free Tom Mooney.

So, with the Bisbee deportations of 1917, when the Phelps-Dodge Copper Company of Arizona, by means of armed thugs, drove out of town into the desert several hundred striking workmen, and the Government dared not punish them. And so, with the persecutions and prosecutions of the I.W.W. — the open, barefaced, shameless

---

[51]Thomas Joseph Mooney (1882-1942) was an American labor leader, convicted of the Preparedness Day bombing in San Francisco in 1916 that left 10 dead and 40 injured. He was eventually pardoned in 1939. (A.K.B.)

crushing of a great labor organization by the capitalist class....

As the class-conscious workers develop political strength, the capitalist parties sink their differences and combine against them; they falsify the ballot; they use the police and the engines of the State to prevent the workers' voting; they gerrymander political districts, so that the majority of the voters get the minority of representatives. The conditions of labor in the United States cause hundreds of thousands of workers to drift from place to place in order to find work — and these workers cannot vote, because of residential qualifications. Poll taxes bar others. The disabilities of aliens, and the difficulties of naturalization — especially at present — disenfranchise thousands more. The anti-syndicalist laws for natives, and the deportation laws for aliens, still further compel silence from all who hold anti-capitalist political and economic opinions.

But after all, the most effective way in which the workers' vote is influenced is by making use of the economic relation between the worker and the employer. The worker is dependent upon the capitalist for his very life — his job. If he does not do as he is told, the worker is deprived of his job, and forced to join the floating army of the unemployed upon which capitalism rests. Now the worker, however high his wages, is squeezed by rent and the cost of living until he is upon the verge of starvation anyway. The shortest illness, the least stoppage of work forces him over the edge into abject poverty. Burdened with a family, the worker cannot afford to quit work; he cannot afford to hold opinions contrary to the boss; he cannot even afford to exercise a vote against his boss's politics.

In Lima, Ohio, a few years ago, there was a municipal election pending. The population of Lima is largely supported by two factories, and the workers were about to elect a Socialist administration. The owners of the two factories thereupon issued a statement to the effect that if the Socialists won, the factories would move away. This would have brought disaster upon the workers, many of whom owned their own homes and had families to support. The Socialist administration was not elected....

In 1916, a Preparedness Parade was held in New York City, which had a great effect upon Congress, because of its size. When the reasons for this mass-demonstration came to be analyzed, however, it was found that most of the workers who marched were forced to do so or lose their jobs. The same phenomenon was more clearly shown throughout the country in the subscriptions to Liberty Loans and the contributions to the Red Cross and other semi-private enterprises. The workers had to pay or be fired, and in some states these financial campaigns were accompanied by terrorization and intimidation at the point of a gun. Thus, the workers were forced to support the political measures of the ruling class by their very dependence upon this ruling class. In an earlier article, I have described how the political power was taken away from the elected officials of the working class Party by the State Councils of National Defense, and how the legislators elected by the Socialists (Berger, the Cleveland Aldermen, etc.) were deprived of their seats in the most cynical manner by the capitalists, and thus Socialist political action was completely nullified.

But all this is nothing to the indirect influence exerted upon the people by the capitalist control of the churches, the schools, and the press. During the war, we have seen very clearly the relation between the great capitalists and the churches and schools. The capitalists give the money which supports the church and pays the minister; which endows the largest universities and pays the professors. In some cases, during the war, the State Councils of Defense threatened ministers who dared to preach against the war; others lost their positions. The same thing is true, in a more glaring degree, of the teachers in schools and universities. The pressure of the capitalist endowments, the Boards of Directors of Churches, and the Overseers of the Universities and Schools, forced teachers and ministers to keep silence, or drove them helpless into a hostile world, where for all practical purposes a complete black-list existed. And since the War has ended, this process of driving out economic and political heretics still goes on, though with increased vigor, under cover of the cry of "Bolshevism." In the public schools and the State Universities, also, the same action takes place, and with even more speed and brutality, owing to the capitalist control of the political machinery. This is supplemented, in cases where it is awkward or inadvisable to invoke the law, by lynchings and mob-violence provoked by Chambers of Commerce and National Security Leagues, and by deliberately falsified "investigations," whose object it is to misrepresent the Labor Movement in such a way as to set the Governmental machinery in motion.

The press is a still more powerful weapon. The control of newspapers, and especially of the popular magazines, has of late years been concentrated in the hands of the great capitalistic interests, who are content even to lose money so long as they control the avenues of public expression. News is practically a monopoly of one great press association, which expresses clearly and faithfully the great capitalist point of view. Editors and reporters who do not conform to this view are discharged and boycotted; a black-list exists.

In this way, news is practically denied to the labor press. The advertisers are leagued not to advertise in radical papers, so as to make it impossible for them to do more than exist. And to cap the climax, the Postmaster-General may exclude from the mails any publication which he sees fit, without giving any reason; thus, entailing immense and often insupportable damage upon the publication and its backers, and preventing the discussion of political and economic questions.

There are those who say, "This is not the fault of political democracy. It is an abuse of democracy, which, if remedied, would permit the free exercise of the ballot to conquer political power." Let it be admitted that these conditions are unusual, and that in normal times there would be more freedom of expression to the Labor Movement. *But that is just the point* — in abnormal times political democracy breaks down, and *it is always abnormal times when the capitalist class fears that the workers may conquer political power.* The open suppression of the political power of the workers is simply an indication of what goes on successfully all the time.

Property is power. Property is political power. Only the abolition of property will ensure the working of real democracy, and only the dictatorship of the proletariat can abolish property.

A majority in Congress and the Supreme Court, without the dictatorship of the proletariat, will not give the workers power. The capitalist class does not control the State because it has a majority in Congress. *It has a majority in Congress, because it controls the machinery of the State*, under the dictatorship of the bourgeoisie.

The industrial era has brought with it a new kind of political action, the action of the masses on the economic field, strikes demonstrations, insurrections. This form of action is well known to us, it is well-established, and even legal. When workers want a raise of wages or a decrease of hours, they do not go to the ballot-box. They go on strike. The pity is that they do not see that this, too, is the way to gain control of the State — a political act — and that this is the only way.

The only power which the capitalist power cannot oppose is the organized and unified action of the proletarian mass.

Suggested Reading

Dearborn, Mary V. *Queen of Bohemia: The Life of Louise Bryant.* New York: Houghton Mifflin Company, 1996.

Eastman, Max. *Heroes I Have Known: Twelve Who Lived Great Lives.* New York: Simon & Schuster, 1942.

Eastman, Max. *Love and Revolution: My Journey Through an Epoch.* New York: Random House, 1964.

Foster, William Z. *History of the Communist Party of the United States.* New York: International Publishers, 1952.

Gelb, Barbara. *So Short a Time: A Biography of John Reed and Louise Bryant.* New York: W.W. Norton & Co., Inc., 1973.

Hicks, Granville. *John Reed: The Making of a Revolutionary.* New York: The MacMillan Company, 1936.

Hovey, Tamara. *John Reed: Witness to Revolution.* Los Angeles: George Sand Books, 1975.

Reed, John. *An Anthology.* Moscow: Progress Publishers, 1966.

Reed, John. *Insurgent Mexico.* New York: International Publishers, 1969.

Reed, John. *Romania during World War I: Observations of an American Journalist.* Las Vegas: Center for Romanian Studies, 2018.

Reed, John. *10 Days that Shook the World.* New York: International Publishers, 1967.

Rosenstone, Robert A. *Romantic Revolutionary: A Biography of John Reed.* New York: Alfred A Knopf, 1975.

Shannon, David A. *The Socialist Party of America: A History.* New York: The MacMillan Company, 1955.

Stuart, John, ed. *The Education of John Reed.* New York: International Publishers, 1955.

Tuck, Jim. *Pancho Villa and John Reed: Two Faces of Romantic Revolution.* Tucson: University of Arizona Press, 1984.

Wolfe, Bertram D. *Strange Communists I Have Known.* New York: Bantam Books, 1967.

Index